Good Pasture
Short & Shorter Stories From Rural Oklahoma

Good Pasture: Short & Shorter Stories From Rural Oklahoma
by Ann S. Oliverio

Cover Design & All Photos: Ann S. Oliverio
Publisher: E on the I Books
ISBN: 978-0-692-78105-0

1. nature 2. autobiography 3. writing 4. essay 5. memoir

First Edition

For Kel & Ike, my constant companions.

Good Pasture: An Introduction *1*

JUNE

How Much I Suck, Or, A Day On A Gun Range in
    Eagle, Colorado   *4*
The Spiral Jetty   *8*
Down the Road Alone   *10*
Beehosting   *11*

JULY

The Painted Bunting   *16*
Dance of the Dragonflies   *17*
I Want To Believe   *18*
Thankful & Thoughtful   *22*
Homemade Dirt   *26*
Do Coyotes Fear the Sound of Fireworks?   *28*
The Road Through Oregon   *30*
It's Good Pasture: Another Oklahoma Gardening Story   *31*
Stray   *34*
The Oracles of Doom   *36*
A Vegan In A Strange Land   *38*
A Trip To the Vet   *40*
Rural Courtesy: The 4-Way Stop & The Wave   *42*
"Dust Can't Kill Me"   *44*
A Scene At Twilight   *47*
The Strenuous Life   *49*
Purple Martins: If You Build It They Will Come   *51*
On Summer Days & Nights Circa 1976   *53*

AUGUST

Wild In The City   *57*
Romancing the Mower   *59*
Taking the Salt Air   *61*
Cloudbusting   *62*
The Loneliness of a Single Shoe on the Highway   *64*
The Sugar House   *66*

In the Stacks   68
Where the Outside Meets the Inside   70
No Life Jackets Allowed: Glen & Bessie Hyde
    Run the Grand Canyon   72
Driving Into Rain   76
Bones and Shells   77
A Town Called I.X.L.   79
One Side of a Conversation   81
A Tall Grayish Figure (Part I)   83
Pictures From A Trip   85
Night Spiders   88
A Tall Grayish Figure (Part II)   90

SEPTEMBER

7 Feet From A Spider   93
Kinds of Flight   96
Working the Seam   99
The Last Halloween   101
Utah State Route 159   103
A Short Work of Fiction (Tilt-A-Whirl)   106
Evening Walks   108
Dizzy Dean Days   110
A Perfect Circle: Goodbye to R.E.M.   112
A Trip Into Town   115

OCTOBER

Sundance, The Point of the Mountain and A Day Away   119
Memories Of A Passenger   123
U.S. Route 50   125
Waiting for Rain   128
The Hackberry Tree   130
A Greenhouse for Winter   131
A Tomb is Opened in Oklahoma   133

NOVEMBER

The Weight Of Loving A Dog   136

The Mockingbird Returns   *138*
The Small Town Myth   *140*
Memories Of Baked Goods Past   *142*
Grief Management   *144*
Some Thoughts About Dirt   *146*
Movies with Mom   *147*

DECEMBER

The Dream   *150*
The Name Begins with the Letter W   *152*
Before It Snows   *154*
The Point of Rocks   *155*
Getting Lost: A Christmas Story   *156*
Lost...And Found   *158*
A Flea in Winter   *159*
Part of the Pack   *161*

JANUARY

Christmas In the Back Country   *164*
A Trip to the DMV   *166*
Handwork   *169*
Running in Places   *171*
Stone Knives & Bear Skins   *172*

FEBRUARY

A Humane Society   *176*
The Long Shadows of Late Afternoon in Winter   *178*
Winter Comes (Briefly) to Oklahoma   *179*
The Body on the Road   *180*
He Looked Like Jesus   *182*

MARCH

Back to My Plow   *186*
Honey Is For Bees   *187*

APRIL

Mom: A Meditation on Life & Memory   *189*

MAY

Hunting Hornworm   *192*

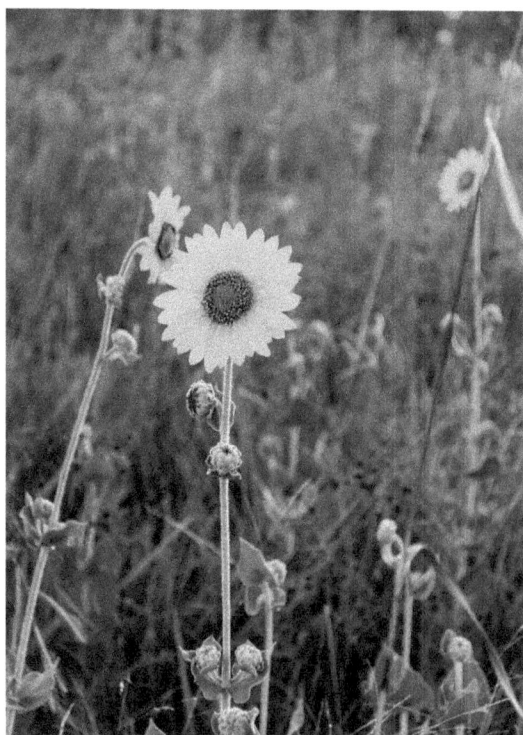

Good Pasture: An Introduction

It's a problem I have or maybe a lack of something. Call that something an absence of focus, ideas, or follow-through, it all comes down to the same thing. I can't write long, detailed stories. Even long *short* stories. I just don't have *it*, whatever that It may be. I have a stack of notebooks filled with tales that start out with great promise and then come to a screeching halt. No climax, no tension, no... ending.

No matter, it turns out. My kind of writing found a home when I discovered and embraced blogging. Blogging became the ideal outlet for my desire to write and was the perfect complement to my inability to write long and complex stories. Oh, and also dialogue. I don't do dialogue.

Most of the short and shorter stories gathered here appeared on my short-lived (see what I did there?) blog called *Dough, Dirt, & Dye: The Essential Elements of My Piece of the Planet*. Dough because I bake bread; dirt because I (used to) garden quite a bit, and dye because I occasionally put my moth-eaten degree in fine arts to use. The stories are divided into months and placed in chronological order.

During the couple of years that I devoted way too many hours on the triple D site, it seemed that I had an endless supply of little stories to tell about my daily life: Ike (our dog), the wisp of a town I call home, cows and coyotes, trees and sunflowers, roads traveled, and stray, disconnected memories that stubbornly stayed in my head. But then one day the well went dry and my passion switched to writing recipes and taking photos of food instead. I miss those days, though, of inspiration and writing more or less freely, of crafting words.

There are also many new (as of 2016) stories here and some

writing that I've "brought over" from my current site, *An Unrefined Vegan* (of the aforementioned recipes and food photos). But for the most part the material is old and dates from 2011-2012. I've cleaned up and reworked many of the stories, most of which are true (though there are a few fictional tidbits here and there). Just for fun. And I've weeded out those stories that really only made sense within the context of a blog. To some stories I've added follow-up comments.

It's been entertaining and educational, going back through those two years. Turns out they were especially hard and heart-breaking ones. They gave me my first taste of true loss. I'm glad to have the written record, but if I could un-write all of the stories to restore my family as I knew it in early 2010, I would not hesitate.

That's the background of this little volume. Welcome to Oklahoma. I hope you enjoy your visit to "my piece of the planet."

Annie
September 2016
Holdenville, Oklahoma

JUNE

How Much I Suck, Or, A Day On A Gun Range in Eagle, Colorado

From the perspective of Rob Pincus, founder of I.C.E. Training, just about anyone who enrolls in one of his "reality based firearm and personal defense" classes sucks at something. And he will, over the course of eight hot, noisy, gritty hours, find out what that something is and peck at it like a crow on a fat pecan until the shell cracks open.

I know because I took the Combat Focus Shooting class and I *did* nearly crack. Seven hours in I was pretty sure I'd had enough. The sun was relentless, and at 6,601 feet, it was that much closer to my skin. My eyes were dry, hands coated in black from handling 400 rounds of 9mm ammunition. Despite reapplying sunscreen at every magazine reload (a.k.a. break), the backs of my arms were burned a bright red. The water I'd brought was no longer even remotely cool and several hours earlier I'd managed to get my left thumb painfully pinched shoving a full magazine into my gun and a tender blood blister had formed.

Yeah, yeah. I can hear the sound of the world's smallest violin playing right about now. Fair enough. But, I'm not looking for sympathy. That was the physical part and well, I kinda dug pushing myself that way and for the same reason I love feeling sore the day after a particularly hard workout.

My body could handle it. It was my *brain* that was fried. What started as a leisurely stroll at the beginning of the day swelled to an intimidating mountain climb by late afternoon. My head was muddled with words of action: move, crouch, reach, draw, grip, push, fire, drop (the empty mag), insert (the full mag), *don't look down at it!*, observe, move, assess, reholster. And do it all over again. And again. And all the while Rob is pecking at the shell. *What are you doing?! Why? Don't do that! Why are you shooting so fast? Why aren't you moving? Where did that last bullet go? Why?! What was the guy next to you doing? Don't do that ever again!*

When Kel and I arrived at the gun range that morning, I thought I'd be the only female taking the course, a beginner's immersion in self-defense with a pistol, but to my relief two other women soon showed up. I had also been concerned that I would be the rank rookie on the range (I was close), but I wasn't. Nevertheless, I was nervous as hell, hands shaking, stomach sour. The day didn't start out so good for me. As I went to push a full magazine into my pistol before heading out to the range for the first time, I heard Rob yelling. "Put that into the holster *now*! *Right now!*" I looked around to see which dope had incurred his wrath so early in the day. And...he was yelling at me. Red-faced and feeling unjustly chastised, I thought to myself, hell, the safety *was on* and there was *no round* in the chamber! Don't have a cow, dude! But something told me to holster the weapon and keep my mouth firmly shut.

With that inauspicious start the group left the shade of the overhang and straggled out, checking gear one more time, putting on hats and sunglasses. The baked, dusty ground of the pistol firing range glittered with spent brass. At the far end a long row of targets stared back at us, patiently waiting to be shot full of holes.

"Reality-based" shooting - or point shooting, is about instinctive practice rather than target-based practice. Training one's body to react the way that it naturally would in a "combat" situation. Our natural instinct when confronted with a threat might be, depending on the circumstances, to turn and run away, or it might be to hunker down and bring up the arms to defend the chest and head, to squarely face the threat and position the body in a way that makes it more compact and steadier to counter a force coming at it. Rob teaches this tactic with a pistol. The gun becomes a natural

5

extension of the arms which are thrusting powerfully out towards the threat, head tucked down, shoulder muscles firm to steady the gun and absorb the recoil of the pistol when fired.

A few months prior to taking Rob's course, a friend gave me a slim book called *Bulleyes Don't Shoot Back: The Complete Textbook of Point Shooting for Close Quarters Combat* by Col. Rex Applegate. In this way I got a nice little primer on what to expect from my day in Eagle. Coincidentally, and months before the class was even on my radar, I'd read *Natural Born Heroes: Mastering the Lost Secrets of Strength and Endurance*, by Christopher McDougall. McDougall writes about two British police officers serving in Shanghai between 1900-1940, William Fairbairn & E.A. Sykes, who pioneered instinctive defense. Col. Applegate, author of *Bulleyes Don't Shoot Back*, began his combat handgun training with these same two gentleman! I love coincidences like this. Having this background info brought an extra dimension to my training with Rob.

But back to that hot and bright and long day in Eagle, CO. A few hours in and after a particularly bad array on my target, Rob asked me what happened and after I replied he barked, *"I want you to think about how much you suck,"* before walking disgustedly (or so I imagined) away from me, leaving me feeling, well, that I actually *did* suck. And not just at the range, but at many things, possibly even at *all things*! I shook off this sobering thought and turned back to the target. Maybe by the end of the day I'd suck a little less. At shooting.

In his classes, Rob pours on the verbal abuse and insists on a fast pace so that both mind and body are stressed. The intention is to mimic as closely as possible what an actual encounter with a "bad guy" might feel like. One has to set aside ego and try to benefit from the experience that Rob

6

has amassed over his years in law enforcement, as an officer in the Army Reserves, and through his years of weapon training.

Looking back, Rob only shamed me a few times and never with criticism or instruction that I didn't deserve or need. Sometimes learning can be ego-busting, embarassing, and as painful as sunburn on the backs of one's arms.

- June 30, 2016

I highly recommend Christopher McDougall's book, *Natural Born Heroes*. It's the truth-is-stranger-than fiction account of misfit British spies and brave Crete natives battling Nazis by means of sabotage, guerilla warfare and their own wits and ingenuity - and how fitness in the 21st Century, such as parkour and Crossfit - is inspired by instinctive and functional movement of the body.

The Spiral Jetty

All we have, it seems to me, is the beauty of art and nature and life and the love which that beauty inspires.

- Edward Abbey, *The Journey Home: Some Words in Defense of the American West*

I don't have a Bucket List of places around the world that I need to see before I shrug off this mortal coil, but deep in the recesses of my mind I do keep a list of sorts. It's a fairly short list of works of art that mean something to me for one reason or another. Over the years I've been able to cross off the majority of the items on this mental list, but one has refused to budge. It is, in fact, geographically the closest piece to me, yet it has remained frustratingly elusive. Until recently, that is.

Strung out along the edge of Rozel Point on the Great Salt Lake in Utah, the earthwork *Spiral Jetty* was created by Robert Smithson over a few week period in April 1970. It's a delicate tendril of basalt rock and salt crystals that curls 1,500 feet out into the sometimes pink, sometimes red waters. Come when the level of the lake is high (as we did) and the spiral nearly disappears. At other times, one can walk onto the lake to the very end of the spiral and turn back to look at the shore and the scrubby brown hills rising away from it.

There is some work, planning and dedication involved in visiting the Jetty, although recent improvements to the gravel road out to the site have made going there relatively easy. But it is in the middle of nowhere. Smithson chose his site perfectly. The isolation and remoteness of the Jetty make it the ideal place for contemplation, reflection, connecting with the natural world or just a pleasant afternoon hike.

Lake and sky blend together at the horizon, the wind is constant. Waves of yellow-green algae sweep along the jumbled surface of the Jetty and salt crystals sparkle among the black rocks as pelicans fly their steady, patient beat high above. Smithson's creation doesn't impose on or overwhelm the surroundings. Though obviously man-made, it feels like a natural extension of the shore (unlike the decaying relic of a true jetty not far from Smithson's Jetty). Spending time with the Jetty is not unlike the feeling one gets from a long, intense yoga session.

Now, after extolling the virtues of this mystical place, I'm going to do my best Edward Abbey imitation by both encouraging you to go see this treasure and...imploring you to stay away. Although it is made of rocks, the Jetty is touchingly fragile. Too many feet will quickly destroy what has endured for the past forty-two years. Not too long ago, Spiral-seekers needed 4-wheel drive, sturdy hiking boots (the last few miles had to be walked) and a true love of art and nature in order to pay homage to Smithson's masterpiece. Now anyone in a low-slung sedan can cruise to the edge of the Jetty, lean out of the car window to snap a photo and speed off again, leaving a plume of light brown desert dust behind him. If you come, come with respect, tread lightly and leave in awe of what nature can inspire in man.

- June 16, 2012

Down the Road Alone

There is a road, no simple highway,
Between the dawn and the dark of night,
And if you go no one may follow,
That path is for your steps alone.

– Ripple by The Grateful Dead

I am blessed. I'm surrounded by beauty and cradled in love. At night the only sound is that of my own breathing: in and out, in and out. Maybe the call of a whippoorwill or the soft hooting of an owl. The air outside smells of warmth and earth and on certain days an indefinable "green." I have a partner who supports me, makes me laugh and forgives my irritable moments, indulges my silliness and my crazy, roving need to create Something. My time is my own. Our animal companion brims with joy and energy and I can feel his love for us in every wiggle and every wet slurp. I am healthy and strong. Indeed, life is beautiful.

But then I remember that I am heading down an unfamiliar road. A road which we will all one day take. If we can, we take the journey for as long as possible with someone at our side, but at a certain point, we go on alone. And then I *know* the other truth. Life is hard.

I'm traveling that road with my beloved brother. My friend. This time, I am the companion and he will continue on alone. I will walk beside him for as long as I can, for as long as it takes. I don't want him to go, but I can do nothing to keep him here.

- June 20, 2012

Beehosting

Kel and I are not beekeepers. We are beehosters. When we moved to Oklahoma we had every intention of being beekeepers. What better complement for our new orchard, flower beds and the vegetable garden that we envisioned? Like expectant parents we bought piles of books and read everything we could about keeping bees, harvesting honey, Colony Collapse Disorder and planting the right flowers to attract our bees to the garden. We read about the different varieties of honeybees and their various strengths and weaknesses. We built hive boxes and painted them bright white. We bought the smoker, the hive tools and the suits with the screened hats. We loaded up on antibiotics and special beeswax sheets so our bees would have fragrantly familiar surfaces on which to build comb.

Finally the big day came: the day we took possession of Our Girls. On a beautiful late afternoon in April, we drove to a nearby town and picked up two boxes of bees sent to us from a Texas apiary. We motored carefully home and after letting the bees rest in the dark and cool of our garage we were ready to "install" our bees into their respective hives. We tried hard to follow the directions on encouraging the bees into their new homes, but we were clumsy and panicky, not realizing that the bees were smarter than we were and would do exactly what they were supposed to do, in their own time, without interference from us. The experience was traumatic for us and also to the bees, I'm sure. But the process went well. All of the bees were in by the next morning, and we congratulated ourselves for accomplishing our first beekeeping task.

After that, we visited our bees frequently throughout the day to marvel at their activity, their petite size and their complete disinterest in us. We would let them crawl on our hands, disdaining the suit and veil. We were the big, benevolent creators bringing them thick sugar syrup to get them through those first early days as they got accustomed to their new digs and before their pollen and nectar gathering reached full swing. A few weeks in we noticed a suspiciously heavy amount of activity around the entrances to the hives. Dark brown bees, not the color we remembered our bees being, swayed and swarmed around the entrance. Having read too much but learned little, one of us sounded the alarm: ROBBING! A beekeeper's nightmare. We were certain we would lose our bees to a barbarian hoard of "wild" bees determined to steal the stocks of honey. We drenched bedsheets in water and draped them over the hives (as one of our books recommended). We constructed small mesh frames designed (we'd read) to deter robber bees but that would not challenge Our Bees who would follow trails of scent into the hive. It was a tense time, but eventually it appeared that our efforts were successful. Later we realized that the robber bees were in all probability *new* bees doing orientation flights around the entrance of the hive so they could fix in their little bee brains where home was. How confusing it must've been for them having wet sheets blocking the entrances!

Then three things happened that turned us from beekeepers to beehosters. 1) While hanging around one of the hives admiring our handiwork and noting how much pollen the bees were carrying on their back legs, an ominous buzzing sound swelled and grew and suddenly a guard bee dive bombed Kel and stung him square on the forehead, sacrificing itself for the safety of the hive. Mission accomplished: we quickly gave the bees their space. 2) A few days later, after my morning run, I decided to visit the Girls and say hello. As I peered into the opening of the hive, two angry bees flew at my head, sending me careening down the driveway as they kept pace, pinging the back of my head. They did not sting me but they did hustle me, arms flailing wildly, to a PR in

12

the 50 yard dash. FYI: bees do not like the smell of sweat (or other harsh scents). And 3) the day finally came when we absolutely had to do a hive inspection. Inspections are supposed to be regular affairs so that the beekeeper can monitor the health and activity of the hive and of the queen. We'd been avoiding it for various valid but also entirely ridiculous reasons. We suited up and after struggling for an hour to get the smoker going, we swallowed hard and faced the hives. Giving them thick whiffs of smoke (which is supposed to put them in mind of a forest fire; the bees get busy ingesting honey to carry off with them in the event they need to rebuild somewhere else and supposedly don't notice us cracking open their home) and gathering our prying tools, we began lifting off the topmost hive box. Honeybees do not like cracks or drafts so they fill them with a formidable cement-like substance. After much exertion, the box began to give and we lifted it off only to discover that the bees had filled every nook and cranny with honeycomb. Honey gushed everywhere dripping onto the ground, onto us, onto the bees crawling frantically around their newly destroyed home. It was a horrible sight. Complete devastation. As quickly as we could, we scraped away the damaged honeycomb, rescued the bees that had gotten mired in honey and closed everything back up again. Reluctantly we performed the same task on the second hive. After that, we were especially loathe to inspect the hives again. It just seemed like way too much stress on us, but more importantly, on the bees.

About this time I ran across a beekeeping site that espoused the "lazy man's" method of beekeeping. Sounded like it was tailor-made for us. The site recommended a very low maintenance plan for caring for honeybees – essentially set them up, feed them when nature's stores get low, but then let them do what they've been doing (and doing well) long before humans started poking, smoking, prying and harvesting. Henceforth it's the plan we've followed and our bees

13

are thriving. We still bring them water on hot days and make sure they have sugar syrup in early spring when their reserves are low but they are otherwise beautifully self-sufficient, pollinating our fruit trees and melons and busily visiting the crape myrtles, the catmint, the clover, the salvia and the lowly dandelion. We have never harvested their honey, but let it remain so that they have the stores to get them through long winters. On warm and sunny winter days they come out and somehow sniff out pollen or nectar to bring back to the hives. When it's rainy or cold they stay indoors like the sensible creatures they are. When it gets very hot, troops of them hang out on their porch, turn their backs to the entrance and fan their wings, sending cooler air into the hive to help their toiling sisters. We still stop by the hives to admire Our Girls. We just do it with a lot more respect (and after we've showered).

- June 29, 2011

JULY

The Painted Bunting

In the early evening, he sits at the very top of a tall Winged Elm tree, bright as a parrot, singing his sweet and simple song to mark and defend his territory. It's a cheery trill, sounding hardly at all like aggression. Sometimes a female can be seen fluttering among the tall grasses below, searching for seeds.

Every year our home becomes the summer retreat of a Painted Bunting or two. They are so reclusive it's hard to know how many may live in the area. How fortunate for our eyes and ears that such an exotic-looking bird (and one commonly captured to keep as a pet in a cage) chooses a plain state like Oklahoma in which to summer. With its bright splashes of red and purple and green it looks better suited to a steamy, vine-rich jungle.

According to Audobon, the numbers of Painted Buntings are slowly declining due to nest predation and the aforementioned pet appeal. No wonder it's a shy bird, one that prefers to stay hidden in dense grass and deep foliage.

The Bunting has become, for us, a harbinger of summer. When he arrives we know that the heat is about to turn on full blast and that we can expect his friends the Scissortail Flycatchers and the Night Jars to arrive shortly. He's also become a welcome part of our evening walks as he serenades our steps up the hill and through the grass.

- July 21, 2016

Dance of the Dragonflies

What draws them to the open space between the back porch and the garden gate? Is it the angle of the early evening sun, so soft and golden or is it the faint coolness radiating up from the grass and earth that inspires the cloud of dragonflies to circle and flutter and wheel so joyously in that last brilliant burst of sunshine before night closes in? Their delicate shimmering wings, their iridescent, top heavy bodies gliding like tiny planes, turning sharply, diving.

Their erratic dance isn't one to celebrate day's end. It's a feeding frenzy. The dragonflies are gorging themselves on the buzzing cloud of tiny insects that circle, mesmerized by something unseen, in tight balls like schools of fish.

- July 23, 2016

For lots and lots of facts on dragonflies, check out Dragonfly-site.com. It describes these exotic-looking, delicate and beloved flying creatures as "killing machines." Gulp.

I Want To Believe

When convention and science offer us no answers, might we not finally turn to the fantastic as a plausibility?

– Fox Mulder, Episode 1, Season 1 of *The X-Files*

Unlike FBI Special Agent Fox Mulder, extraterrestrials are not my thing. I am not fascinated by the existence of other beings who may or may not be visiting us from their worlds (performing hideous experiments on us). It's the world that shadows our own that I find interesting. Another plane, another dimension, the spirit world.

I have a very gentle ghost story to tell. But first, meet me, the skeptic. I am not a religious person, nor do I consider myself spiritual or even superstitious. Black cats are just sweet felines and I've walked under a ladder or two to no ill effect. Even as a child I knew that the Brothers Grimm's stories that I loved were morality tales and not about ogres and witches. There was never a pot of gold at the rainbow's end and the sinister genie that visited my childhood dreams couldn't really hurt me. I was and am a very practical person who searches for the down-to-earth explanation for things. Yet some of my experiences have defied logical explanations. Once, as a preteen, my siblings and cousins and I lifted one of us several inches off of the floor with only our fingertips and the chanting of, over and over, "stiff as a board, light as a feather." Laugh if you will, but it worked* and it scared the shit out of us. What about those ethereal strands of shimmering light that floated past me while out for a walk one summer evening? Or the time a scruffy, bearded man walked out of the Nevada desert in the middle of the night to help my brothers and me bring a dead car back to life?

It's not as if I haven't had opportunities. I spent my childhood sleeping in a bedroom where a woman had died in a fire, yet I never once felt even the slightest ripple from her

18

spirit. For several summers, I made trips to the Lilydale Assembly in New York State to sit in on "message services" where mediums call out to audience members with greetings, advice or warnings from those who have passed on. Each time I attended I eagerly awaited my message, but none came. Surely somebody out there wanted to share *something* with me? Kel went to Lilydale once with me and was called on twice. So either there is no "there" there, or I have a protective shell, a kind of spirit-resistant lead coating, perhaps, that deflects contact from beyond. Despite my apparent lack of spiritual attraction and my innate skepticism I can acknowledge this, however: I don't know. I don't know how we got here, I don't know what's "out there" and I don't know what happens to us after we slip away forever from our loved ones.

Now, for the ghost story. Sometime very late on May 12 or perhaps when it was just barely May 13, long after even the crickets had quieted, I was still unable to sleep. I couldn't get comfortable. Thoughts raced in and out of my head. I had a lump in my throat. I was hot and then chilled. I finally settled into a comfortable position and then – as happens when our minds drift and calm – my sense of time and place slipped away. I wasn't in any *place*. My brother was in front of me. I asked him if I could hug him and then I felt him in my arms. I could feel the weight of his chest against mine, feel his strength and solidity. His realness. My fingers rested atop the muscles of his back. I placed my head on his shoulder and he rested his on mine and as he did, I heard the words, *I love you, Ann.* I don't say that he whispered them because that isn't right. It was what I heard and felt, soft and quiet. Not sound as I understand it in the waking world. And then all of a sudden, I caught a glimpse of something rushing by me, just at the edge of sight. It slipped by me so quickly. Then my arms were empty, truly empty. My brother was gone. I woke up or perhaps my level of consciousness changed and my first thought was: he was here. It felt

19

so true. I fell asleep knowing he had visited me. Since his death, I've had many dreams about my brother, but this was unlike any dream I'd had. The frightening thing about an experience like this isn't the idea that some essence of my brother is roaming the ether, it is the thought that it may never happen again. What if that was the one and only time I again feel his presence? If so, then it will be just one more thing about him to miss.

It's not much of a ghost story, is it? Later, in the light of day, my practical and skeptical side offered explanations about what had occurred. My brother's visit could have been a vision produced by the anti-inflammatory drug I was then taking for a shoulder injury. The warning label was about a mile long and quite possibly hallucinations were one of the many side effects. Perhaps it was a dream offered up by my restless and grieving mind as a means of comforting itself and me. Our minds are so powerful that they sometimes show the eye something that isn't really there, like the day I saw a baby reaching up its tiny arm as it lay in the middle of a busy road. I lurched towards it and when I looked again there was no baby. Just a crumpled brown bag being blown about.

So, no, I don't believe the adage that seeing is believing. But feeling something, having one's arms around it, that's real. I felt my brother. So maybe my lead coating isn't impervious. Maybe my brother had found a way to reach across the murky twilight between the living and the dead to put his arms around me and to let me know that he loved me. This is what I want to believe.

Charles Andrew Oliverio
February 13, 1961 – July 5, 2012

Suggested reading for my fellow skeptics:
Spook, by Mary Roach

Incognito: The Secret Lives of the Brain, by David Eagleman

The Believing Brain: From Ghosts and Gods to Politics and Conspiracies—How We Construct Beliefs and Reinforce Them as Truths, by Michael Shermer

- July 5, 2013

*I have since learned how this supposed miracle works, thanks to psychic phenomena debunker, James "The Great" Randi. You can learn, too, by reading his book, *Flim-Flam! Psychics, ESP, Unicorns & Other Delusions.*

Thankful & Thoughtful

The things alive do not know the secret... Of late years, however, I have come to suspect that the mystery may just as well be solved in a carved and intricate seed case out of which life has flown, as in the seed itself.

– Loren Eiseley, *The Immense Journey*

My brother died at 3:25 a.m. on July 5. The pop and sizzle of neighbors' firecrackers kept him company that night, gray skies and a gentle rain in the morning broke the spell of heat and drought and sun, more soothing than melancholy. As determined and independent in his dying days as he was as a vibrant, healthy man, I have no doubt his plan was to make it through July 4. July was his favorite month and Independence Day his favorite holiday.

In the hours and days after his death, little things took on weighted importance: the memory of the last meal together at a restaurant; the image of a sweet smile when at last voice and words, but not comprehension, were taken from him; the half-full glass of water by his bed; the backpack on the kitchen table containing bottles of aspirin, ear plugs and a bathing suit from the last trip he took (to California); the tube of toothpaste, indented in the middle by the squeeze of his hand; his beat-up work boots looking as if he'd stepped out of them mere moments before. It is those things more than the profound and sobering permanence of passing that make me break down. What is more poignant than the little, seemingly insignificant objects and moments that make up a human life?

Anyone who has suffered through an illness or has helped a family member or friend knows that it is not a solo project. It is a team effort requiring tens of supporting and supportive roles. And so I have many people to thank. First and foremost among them, my family. My mom and dad dug deep and called on reserves that any 20-year old would envy.

Their strength and dignity through that lonesome night of loss is an example I will carry with me until my own end comes. My other brother whose advise and care steadied during moments of stress and uncertainty. My sister was a rock, holding firm during times when I melted like a candle. Love to my partner, Kel, for keeping the home fires stoked and for caring for our little (furry) one, Ike. Kel's support has never wavered. He loved my brother. The caring embrace of extended family was felt over the long miles.

It is impossible to imagine what this process would have been like without the guidance, knowledge and compassion of our hospice team. There were many late night visits and phone calls, moments of doubt and fear made manageable by a comforting voice on the other end of the line. Stacey, Robyn and Carolyn guided us down that very difficult road. Special gratitude goes to John, the gentle aide who helped my brother maintain his pride and dignity up to that very last day of life. We were also fortunate to meet Riley, a young man who made our nights easier by his patient presence and his willingness to be touched by a family's saddest hours.

Thanks and love go to the many friends – old and new, near and far – who sent emails and called. In challenging times, the true and the false are shown in stark relief. Some of my brother's friends reached lovingly out to us, shared aspects of him we never knew and offered to help in any way that they could. Fate or coincidence sent Somer into my life at just the right moment. She shared her huge, loving, nurturing heart with my brother, but also loaded the back of her vehicle – several times – with plant-based deliciousness and made the trek to Bountiful to spend time with me and open her arms for much-needed hugs. Her beautiful kids never failed to cheer me with their exuberance and their life and energy. Along with her friends Amanda and Erika (who at the time of this writing had never met me, by the way) she provided heart, soul, and stomach nourishment.

In a strange twist, Faye came into my life on the very day
my brother died and at the same coffee shop where he and
I would go after his appointments at the clinic. Over mu-
tual admiration for short haircuts, I learned that Faye has
the same type of brain cancer as my brother. I'm not one to
linger long on the oddities the universe occasionally throws
across my path, but one would have to be devoid of imagination not to think something rather huge was up. I hope to
spend more time with Faye and to share with her the thin
threads of knowledge I've gathered over the past couple of
years.

Merck and Genentech earned my gratitude for providing
their prohibitively costly chemo drugs gratis through their
assistance programs. Big pharmaceuticals aren't all bad.
Novocure not only earns thanks for pursuing unconven-
tional cancer treatment options, but I'm indebted to them
for giving my brother – free – their Novocure TTF helmet,
an alternative treatment using electric fields to disrupt
cancer cell growth. Dr. Santosh Kesari at his lab at UCSD
prescribed the device and he also, up until the last weeks of
my brother's life, suggested other treatment options. Thank
goodness for all of those, like Dr. Kesari, who dedicate their
lives to eradicating brain cancer.

Lastly, thanks to my brother's medical team at The Hunts-
man Cancer Institute, especially to sweet Crelley who has
become a friend, and Sean, who spent hours with me on
the phone over the past two years explaining complex is-
sues and trying to figure out what made my brother tick.
From the beginning of this journey they provided hope and
knowledge and gave my brother another year of life when
all seemed lost on bleak November days in 2010. I often
wonder how they can work day after day knowing that many
of their patients will live only a short time post-diagnosis.

I am grateful there are people willing to devote their lives to treating such a formidable disease. May a cure be found soon.

- July 16, 2012

I did spend time with Faye. She was one of a kind. An animal lover and defender, a woman with an amazing and inspiring personal history, she seemed to know *every*one in Salt Lake City. She was sweet and strong yet vulnerable and funny as hell. Sadly, Faye passed away less than a year after Charles. She was surrounded by loving family and friends and will be greatly missed by all who knew her.

Homemade Dirt

My partner, Kel, years ago was a city dweller, as I was, and though being a city dweller in a compact D.C. townhouse he used every outdoor nook and cranny not covered in cement to grow things: figs, lemon, apple and pear trees, tomatoes and peppers. He also composted. He was way ahead of his time, "green" speaking.

We met in late summer and by fall he could be heard muttering about "brown gold." How there was so much "brown gold" going to waste all over the city streets. I thought he was seriously off of his nut until he explained that brown gold was the bounty of fallen leaves packed into black plastic garbage bags, ready for trash day, that lined the streets of D.C. It was incomprehensible to him that people actually considered this stuff garbage. He'd drive around the streets, stop and cram bags into his small 2-door Acura until there was only space for himself in the driver's seat.

Now we have 160 acres. Not an inch of it is paved and we can grow anything we want. And we compost. All of our produce scraps get thrown into a sturdy green bucket and it's taken outside to be dug into wherever the compost pile happens to be at that moment. Kel moves it around based on reasons that do not need to be understood by me but are perfectly clear to him. That's how it should be. I provide the organic material and he puts it where it needs to go. Right now the compost lives at one end of the row of tomatoes and it's covered in a thick sheet of black plastic. He gives the compost fresh air now and then, turns it with a pitch fork or shovel and adds the kitchen scraps, cuttings from the garden, spent coffee grounds, a bag of flour gone bad...if it's organic, it gets added to the mix. A faint odor of musty cabbage emanates from it. The pile is a growing mystery. Whatever is underneath the plastic just may get up and walk one day. But for sure, one day, it will be dirt.

As for "brown gold," we have it here, too. Lots of it. Here we use the leaves (mostly scrub, pin and black jack oak) as a protective mulch around the base of other trees, on the asparagus bed and blueberry bushes, or we dig them into the compost pile. The leaves attract earthworms and the earthworms aerate the composting leaves and assist with breaking them down. And then one day, you have, miraculously, dirt. Which goes into the flower and vegetable beds. Amazing.

We've even been known to foray into town during the fall, looking for bags of leaves left for the garbage man. A few of our neighbors, knowing how we covet fallen leaves, collect what they rake from their yards and bring the bags around to us. They probably think we are seriously off of our nuts, but that's alright. It's worth it for the gold.

- July 3, 2011

Do Coyotes Fear the Sound of Fireworks?

What's the matter? Coyote get your deer?

- bumper sticker, via Edward Abbey

All along the back roads and state routes of Oklahoma, small shacks and trailer homes are painted with exploding rockets and bursting stars on the otherwise faded siding. Shuttered throughout most of the year, the shacks come to life in the weeks leading up to July 4. They sell fireworks. During the long holiday weekend, faraway booms can be heard and occasionally, off in the distance, we see flashes in the sky as bright beads of sparks soar, flare briefly and fall to earth as tiny dark spots.

Today I'm thinking about coyotes. I'm thinking about the young family of coyotes living somewhere to the north of us, in the woods, or maybe to the west of us - who knows - in the grassy hollows, in a large den dug into the roots of a big tree. With any luck there are coyote families in both places.

Do coyotes fear the sound of fireworks the way my family dog, Violet, did, running to find the nearest dark place to hide? Or do they just howl in response the way they do when a train whistle blows? Maybe the sounds resemble the sound of a shotgun, in which case, they know to run and hide.

There are a lot of folks in Oklahoma who hate coyotes more than just about anything. Coyotes are routinely shot, poisoned and trapped. Some cretins even hang the limp and lifeless bodies from barbed wire fences, a ridiculous, futile warning to other four-legged interlopers. As if coyotes recognize fences and property lines. Or maybe it's misplaced pride in their kill. Ranchers say that coyotes kill their calves and I say coyotes mostly eat rodents and only cull out the ill or the dying among cattle, performing a needed function on the range. Ranchers complain that coyote lovers always rely on emotion-based logic and we coyote defenders fume that ranchers use a myopic price-per-head-of-cattle reasoning. So the same arguments spin out over and over and over again and coyotes keep getting shot and hung from barbed wire fences.

What I know is that coyotes are safe on our land. I wish I could communicate that to the coyote family, tell them to stay here, that I welcome their hunting and their howls and yips in the night when I'm woken from my dreams to hear them. I appreciate their loping, confident trots across our fields, quick but unhurried when I'm fortunate enough to catch a glimpse of one.

- July 4, 2011

As I work on this volume in July 2016, Kel and I are feeding two tiny coyote pups that have been orphaned through some unknown event. The photo at the beginning of this chapter is of one of the pups, taken by a game camera near where we leave food and water.

The Road Through Oregon

In the early '90s I made the obligatory journey of the searching soul, the directionless youth, the dreamer, otherwise known as the recently-graduated: a cross-country road trip to the land of the endless summer. The car was packed with all of my worldly possessions and I had high hopes for a new and exciting life in northern California.

Reality hit pretty hard and pretty quickly. I knew California was not for me. Knowing of my distress, two good friends offered me a temporary refuge of sorts and asked me to visit them over Thanksgiving. A place to get my head straight, figure out my next move. So I ran away, at least briefly, and drove up to Tacoma, Washington.

My trusty, nine-lived car (a two-door white Hyundai Excel hatchback) and I motored onto I-5, atlas on the seat next to me, a pile of cassette tapes at my fingertips. Now so many years later, there isn't a lot from that journey north that I remember. I was focusing on getting to Tacoma as quickly as I could. But I do remember the deep and inviting green of Oregon. The highway at times cut between mossy mountains misted with wisps of fog. Moisture was everywhere, was on everything. There were tantalizing glimpses of houses among the thick of the trees. The swooshing sound of tires on wet road. The deep greens and soft grays of the landscape felt comforting to my eyes. It all struck me as fresh and clean and I envied those people living among the tall pines and hills. It seemed like a good place in which to run away, to hide from the world and get one's head straight.

- July 6, 2011

It's Good Pasture: Another Oklahoma Gardening Story

On Christmas Day in 2007, Kel and I were still planting fruit trees, the last six lifeless-looking twigs before we could pack up the car and drive east to spend some of the holiday with my parents. We'd been busy planting over 80 fruit trees: apple, cherry, apricot, nectarine, peach and pear for the past week. Kel had been digging holes for weeks before that and I'd put together large chicken wire cages to go around the trees in an attempt to keep gophers from eating the tender, tempting roots.

I don't know about Kel, but I was already imagining the trees when they were mature. Fruit hanging down, more fruit than we could possibly eat and sturdy branches reaching up and out, creating a shady canopy over the entire orchard. Probably Kel was thinking the same thing. He'd had a dream of cultivating his own orchard ever since he was a kid and had spent a summer with his uncle in Indiana. A neighbor had an orchard and Kel was free to pick and eat as much fruit as he wanted. It seemed magical.

A few weeks after we finished planting, we sat out in the orchard with Mrs. C., a friend, neighbor and cattlewoman. A native Oklahoman. We were showing off our hard work. In her slow and considered way, she surveyed the thin, branchless twigs stuck into the ground in neat rows and at the grass, thick and bright green even in January, settled back into her lawn chair and said, just loud enough to hear, "*Sure is good pasture, though.*"

We chuckled about her comment as later we chuckled when an Oklahoma beekeeper told us how he once had an orchard but that he'd given up on it long ago. Too much work that resulted in disappointing results. What did born and bred Oklahomans know about orchards anyway? Turns out they know a lot. They know what not to grow in Oklahoma.

The first spring our trees leafed out and branches magically appeared. They grew like crazy. The second year we had a wet spring and the pear trees were hit with fire blight. We lost a tree or two, but figured that was all part of the deal. Later that same year we noticed bright orange spots on the otherwise perfect leaves of the apple trees. Cedar Apple Rust. Recommendations were to remove all cedar trees in the area (a Sisyphaen task) and to spray the leaves with a copper solution. There went our idea of a pesticide- and herbicide-free orchard.

Yet somehow the fruit trees continued to grow; they looked pretty good. We started to see some fruit coming on the apple trees and that aroused the interest of other kinds of pests. Birds started pecking the young fruit even before it was ripe. Raccoons and opossums climbed the trees and pulled off the fruit, breaking branches and bending my chicken wire cages. One year deer stripped off every single piece of fruit on every single apple tree in one night despite the 6-foot high electrified fence surrounding the trees. Leafrollers chewed the branches completely bare of leaves. And this year, there's no rain.

So the question now for us is: when do we call it quits? When does the time expenditure and heartache outweigh the payoff? I haven't made one pie from the apples or cherries. Kel not once has been able to walk into his orchard and pluck a perfectly ripe, unblemished piece of fruit off of one of the trees. Yet thinking about abandoning the orchard completely is painful. Letting go of a life-long dream is painful. And they are trees after all, beautiful trees. They were just planted by a couple of rubes in the wrong state.

A long time ago, farmers used to grow peanuts in Oklahoma. There are still some acres of corn being cultivated (corn is just big grass, right?). Some people are trying their hands at growing grapes for local wineries. But you don't see orchards here and there's a good reason for that. Oklahoma is just good pasture.

- July 7, 2011

Stray

Maybe it's not a phenomenon particular to Oklahoma or even to rural areas, but just about everyone we know out here has had it happen. The day dawns like any other and then the next moment a dog (or cat) saunters up your driveway and *boom!* you're a pet owner. I don't know if there's an official name for it (other than some obvious choices: lousy, cruel, pathetic, heartless, cowardly), but I call it pet-dumping.

For nearly four years now we've dodged that particular bullet. We've come close a couple of times. A black and white cat seemed interested in finding out if we would be the recipient of its time and attention. We failed its obscure test and the cat moved across the street. And then two dogs appeared one freezing winter morning and were in no hurry to leave. They had collars but no tags. We bought a jumbo bag of Ol' Roy, bowls and a brush. The next day we drove around the area leaving fliers in mailboxes asking if anyone was missing their dogs. No one called us. (Go figure.) They were great dogs, followed us everywhere, barked when they should have and were quiet when they were supposed to be quiet. Then one morning they were gone. No goodbyes, no thank you note.

Yesterday when I got home from running errands in town, I saw a small black dog hugging Kel's heels as if his very life depended on it. My exact thought was this: *that is the ugliest dog I've ever seen.* I assumed it was one of the neighbor's seven dogs that I just hadn't seen before. No such luck.

It's a full day later and we still have a small black dog hugging Kel's heels - and mine when Kel escapes for a few minutes. He's a sweet dog, a puppy still, loving, gentle and obedient. Someone obviously spent time with him, trained him. Now we have another giant bag of Ol' Roy and the bowls have been pressed back into service. Can't find the brush. He is wiggling his way into our hearts. We let him sleep in the garage last night and later I need to head back into town and see about getting some treats, maybe a toy for him to chew on. He'd like that, I think. Will we keep him? We haven't decided yet. Maybe the better question is, will he keep us?

- July 10, 2011

The Oracles of Doom

There are a couple of guys we know – old-timers, locals. In another time and place they might've been called townies. They're good guys. Honest. Hardworking. I affectionately call them The Oracles of Doom.

I can picture them in their faded yet clean and pressed overalls, in their crisp white button downs and tidy Justin boots, sitting in the local diner (or the other local diner, or the other one just down the road from that one) with their cups of bitter black coffee cooling to lukewarm, discussing the latest crisis to befall the town, the county, the state, the country.

In general, nothing is good. Meth addicts are everywhere; break-ins are rampant, petty theft a given. Jobs are scarce and those that are available go unfilled because kids today would rather collect welfare than break a sweat. Anyway, they couldn't pass a drug test. If it's winter it might be that the ponds have frozen up leaving cattle without water or maybe an ice storm has taken down the power lines. Sure hope you remembered to buy propane back in August while the prices were low. Spring is always too short and in summer there is either too much rain or too little of it.

This year if you were smart you sold your cattle a few months back, right after you realized that it was a dry spring and would only be a drier summer. You should probably also cut your losses and disc in the vegetable garden and the feed corn. No sense pouring good water in after bad. You couldn't possibly water them enough this year. Forget about getting a second cutting of hay off of that field of yours and say goodbye to that little bit of money you saved up, because you'll need it to buy bags of creep to keep the cattle fed all winter. Of course, the price of beef is so low you won't make any money when you sell them anyway. Have you noticed that there are a lot more grasshoppers this year?

Hasn't been this bad since 1980. Don't even want to talk about the ticks.

It's easy to get pulled into the gloom, the seeming hopelessness of it all. Especially when air conditioned stir-craziness sets in brought on by being trapped inside day after day due to the 100+ degree temperatures. Perspective is the thing. Fall is coming (with its own problems, of course). I have to remind myself that it wouldn't matter if conditions were perfect. Crops vigorous, cows fat and happy, an equal mix of nourishing rain and gentle sunshine, upstanding townspeople and high-paying jobs galore, The Oracles of Doom would find something negative on which to gnaw over their lukewarm cups of coffee.

- July 12, 2011

A Vegan In A Strange Land

There are three grocery stores in town. One I've never visited. The bars on the windows are a just a tad off putting. One has aisles stacked high with generic label merchandise with names that mimic big brands (*Fruiti-Os!*) but is reliable for having cilantro. Then there's the other one, the one that I go to fairly regularly.

Soon after we'd moved here, we went to this store, detailed list in hand, optimistic. I was doing pretty well until I came to tofu. I looked in the produce section and the dairy section. I didn't bother trying to find a "health food" aisle. Kel suggested I ask someone, but I have a real loathing of asking for help in stores. So I'd decided that they didn't have tofu and I'd just strike that meal off of the menu. Finished, we rolled up the cart to the check-out lane, tofu-less. We queued up, putting our items on the small counter, a couple of people lining up behind us. Then Kel did the unthinkable. Acting on his own initiative with absolutely no encouragement from me, he leaned over to the cashier and with his next words, sealed our fate forever as the town's wacko treehuggers:

"Do you carry tofu?"

Blank stare, long silence from the female cashier before she turned to the neighboring cashier and asked, "Do we carry tofu?"

This produced a frown from the other cashier who cocked her head and bellowed, "Soul food? Do we carry SOUL food?" Every head in the market turned our way.

A few weeks after that, I noticed four boxes of tofu sitting in a basket in the produce section, the unrefrigerated part of the produce section. The boxes had puffed up and appeared to be about to burst. I did not buy any tofu that day. After that I never saw tofu there again.

That's a few years back now and we're more or less regulars, accepted as being a little bit different when it comes to food. The Soul Food cashier never fails to say, "Still eatin' healthy I see," as she scans the soy milk, fruit and veggies from our cart. And I always reply, "Well, we try."

- July 13, 2011

A Trip To the Vet

The vet in town is just about three miles from us and has a mailbox painted to look like a Guernsey cow, full pink udder on the bottom and a fraying rope tail at the back. There's a small stable surrounded by fenced pasture and there are always a few horses nosing around the grass and one or two cows, occasionally a donkey or mule. Once as we drove by a brown calf got loose and we watched for a few minutes while a young cowboy tried in vain to shoo him back inside the fence. Calves can be fast and slippery when they spy fresh grass just outside the barbed wire.

Yesterday we took our vagabond puppy (temporarily named Blunder) to see the vet, to get his shots, find out how old he is and maybe what strange mangling of breeds he might be. Our little guy did beautifully. Took to a leash like it was an expensive necklace to be shown off, wandered around the waiting room investigating corners and under chairs, sat down in front of a woman who came in and waited for her to rub his head.

When the vet came out I was happy to see he looked the way a good country vet ought to – kind eyes, ginger-colored hair washing out to gray, baseball cap, dark blue coveralls a little tight in the middle and a gruff-but-reassuring Oklahoma drawl. He handled Blunder with firm but gentle hands, administering the shots so fast that none of us even noticed. Blunder didn't bark, yip or nip once, despite the manhandling.

The vet told us that Blunder is about 3 months old, can eat as much as he wants (but don't bother with that expensive canned food), and is probably part Dachshund and part bird dog. He chuckled when he said that last. The long, stout body of a Dachshund paired with the short ears and small head of a bird dog struck him as funny, I guess. It's true that our pup has a tendency to lift a front paw and more or less point in the general direction of something. When he commented on the size of the front paws (huge) I asked if that meant he'd grow taller or longer and he replied, "Yes." And laughed again.

So now we know a little more. But what I'd really like to know is what we will never know: what is this dog's story? Where did he come from and how on earth did he find us, so far off of the road and through a thick stand of trees and underbrush to traverse before coming close to the house? And could we really possibly doom him with the name Blunder?

- July 15, 2011

Thank goodness we came up with a better name than Blunder. With all due respect to the vet, as to Ike's pedigree, we think that yes, he's part Dachshund, but rather than bird dog, he's got Labrador Retriever in him.

Rural Courtesy: The 4-Way Stop & The Wave

When I moved here from the city, I brought my city driving with me. The impatience, the quickness to largely unwarranted anger, the belief that everyone else was a bad driver. But city driving doesn't belong here. Going at or over the speed limit is plain bad form (unless you're under 25 years of age). The solid yellow line is just a suggestion and driving on the wrong side of the road is forgivable. But there's another difference here. Time slows at four-way stops. There's some kind of wrinkle that occurs when four stop signs are pounded into place next to two roads crossing each other. The effort it takes to overcome the inertia of a car at rest becomes monumental.

Here's how it plays out: you come to a four-way stop and maybe there's one other car or two other cars to your right, left or across from you. Clearly they arrived at the intersection first and in fact, it looks as if they've been there for some time. You wonder whether or not they are even looking at the road, wonder if they are aware that they've left their driveway.

That's when time begins to shudder to a standstill. Your fellow driver leans back in the seat, scooching down in to get a little more comfortable, hands resting patiently at 10-and-2 on the steering wheel, eyes staring off into the distance, into some memory about which you'll never know. Maybe they are mentally writing a shopping list, a poem, a novel or they're lost in a song playing on the radio. Then they nod at you, real slow-like. They raise their hand up through the molasses of their own lethargy and sweep it in front of them, giving you the go-ahead. You find yourself a bit dazed and with great effort you press on a gas pedal gone spongy and haul yourself and the car through the intersection. As you look in the rearview mirror you see your intersection-friend, a courteous stranger, still sitting, idling next to his stop sign.

This move is closely related to the wave. Drive down any road around here and pass another car and you are almost guaranteed to get some kind of acknowledgement. It might be the full wave - hand completely off of the steering wheel, big and friendly and open as the sky above; or it might be the non-committal four-fingered wave, thumb still wrapped firmly around the wheel or finally, the passive one-fingered wave for those harboring some suspicions about you or maybe they're just conserving as much energy as possible for sitting at the upcoming four-way stop. Often this last wave is so difficult to notice that you have no time to respond with your own wave and you end up gesturing to the empty road in front of you. It leaves you feeling a little bit guilty, a little bit like an unfriendly neighbor.

After four years on these roads, my driving has toned down, become countrified. I still have moments of frustration with my fellow drivers, but it sure is nice to see some courtesy offered to a stranger, a wave between us as we pass, a nod at a four-way stop letting me know I can just go on ahead, there's no hurry.

- July 16, 2011

"Dust Can't Kill Me"

Go to the post office, Walmart, the hardware store, anywhere where people gather and we all want to talk about the heat. Someone in town said that we are over 26 days in a row of 100+ degree temperatures. Starts to make one think. The conditions outside of the air-conditioned comfort of our house are ominous. Leaves shriveling, grass crunching, one of our ponds about dried up. The cracks in the pastures, along the garden beds, running through the brick walkway, are growing into deep and dark fissures. To get from one side to the other we'll soon need ladders laid across them, like traversing the Khumbu Icefalls at Everest.

Kel and I talk about The Dust Bowl relative to our own situation and laugh, but shallowly and without much humor. Stories about the recent dust storms in Arizona don't help. The Dust Bowl is part of the collective memory of Oklahomans, native-born or transplant. The former owner of our ranch was a child during that time. He and his family left Oklahoma for California to escape the conditions and look for work. Okies who weren't even alive during that time share stories that sound like fresh and sore memories.

Most of us know three things about Oklahoma: there are lots of tornadoes, it is mostly flat, and it was Dust Bowl central. There is a sensitivity here to weather phenomena and every unusually dry and hot season carries the potential for becoming the catalyst for catastrophe. Oklahoma's reputation for wind is well-deserved. It either blows torch-hot or bitterly cold. It can feel like a freight train sweeping unfettered from the Gulf straight up through Texas and across the flat geography of the state and the wind sometimes doesn't stop for days. When it's whipping you can't hear yourself think let alone what the person next to you is saying. What the tornadoes don't carry away, the unceasing winds will coat with dirt. On the plus side, out in the panhandle, acres of windmills spread across the open land, taking the wind, making energy.

The voice of The Dust Bowl, Woody Guthrie, was born in a small town not too far from us. Okemah boasts a tidy main street with a memorial dedicated to Guthrie and an annual festival in his honor. Guthrie is inextricably linked with The Dust Bowl and the Great Depression. As a teenager I read *Bound for Glory* and loved it while (happily) missing most of its social and political overtones. I just enjoyed his writing and story. Not long afterwards I bought his *The Dust Bowl Ballads*. It was pretty rough going. I appreciate the spirit of the songs, but I find them hard to listen to. They are sparse and plaintive, evocative of so much sadness and despair and I have a difficult time relating. It was so long ago.

A more resonant accounting for me was reading *The Worst Hard Time* by Timothy Egan, which chronicles individual stories of survival (and not) from those who experienced The Dust Bowl. Most of it is hard to believe, the pictures fantastical. I knew that the Great Plains suffered, but the rest of the country was not immune. In May 1934:

…a flock of whirlwinds started up in the northern prairie…Carrying three tons of dust for every American alive, the formation moved over

the Midwest. It covered Chicago at night, dumping an estimated six thousand tons…By morning, the dust fell like snow over Boston and Scranton, and then New York slipped under partial darkness. Now the storm was measured at 1,800 miles wide, a rectangle of dust from the Great Plains to the Atlantic, weighing 350 million tons.

If your Dust Bowl history is a little sketchy it's a book worth reading. My guess is there are plenty of Okies right now worrying, saying goodbye to their crops for this year, re-membering the stories their mothers and fathers told them, hoping for relief in the form of thick clouds that are full of moisture; that it will rain for a few days straight and refill stagnant ponds and refresh the land. I'm worried, too, but feel that the heat and dry will eventually break and although the cracks and splits in the ground look bad, and though the southern wind and cloudless sky only serve to exacerbate conditions, the roots in the prairie are deep and will keep the earth from blowing east.

- July 22, 2011

A Scene At Twilight

The heifer was still there, lying in the grass, slowly chewing, as the sun dropped behind the dark wall of woods. She watched us as we walked westward and then again later as we returned, walking downhill and east. Earlier we'd seen the rest of the herd, far off in the southern pasture, dots of caramel brown, black, weathered bone, but now her companions had disappeared, leaving her where she'd been for most of the day. Her dark brown skin must've been a sponge for the heat, but she didn't seem to mind, and now as the day reluctantly cooled, the color of her coat and the brown of the dry grass merged into the gray scale of dusk.

When we looked back, we saw that she'd gotten to her feet and was facing in our direction. Slowly she walked towards us and towards the barbed wire gate that leads to water. Kel went to open it and I sprinted to the pump so that I could begin to fill the deep black trough. As Kel unlatched the gate and moved into the small paddock near the house, she ambled behind him, like a dog on a long leash. She made her way slowly to the trough and dipped her head down, pulling the water into her in long drags. We could hear the sound of the water being sucked into her body. When she lifted her head to breathe, long strings of water poured off of her muzzle and dripped back into the trough. She watched us; she watched the dog sniffing around in the grass.

Kel and I sat on the driveway across from her, giving her some distance, the stored heat from the pavement seeping into us. Guinea fowls chattered somewhere far off, their sound like a dozen screen doors badly in need of oil, opening and closing, opening and closing. At some point the buzzing of the cicadas dwindled and ceased. Water dripped from the spigot onto the grass. The dog turned to bite savagely at its tail and the sky changed from pale lavender to a tired gray, like white socks washed with the dark load. The young cow stood at the trough until the leaves were finally drained of their color and the rounded edges of the sky grew darker, then she turned and headed back towards the pasture and her herd.

- July 24, 2011

The Strenuous Life

In the last analysis a healthy state can exist only when the men and women who make it up lead clean, vigorous, healthy lives; when the children are so trained that they shall endeavor, not to shirk difficulties, but to overcome them; not to seek ease, but to know how to wrest triumph from toil and risk.

- From the speech *The Strenuous Life*, April 10, 1899, Theodore Roosevelt

Theodore Roosevelt's idea of the strenuous life involved bagging exotic animal specimens, thundering after cattle in North Dakota on a horse, charging San Juan Hill in Cuba and not letting a bullet fired into his chest put a halt to finishing a speech in Milwaukee. Admittedly he meant much more than all of those things in his famous speech, *The Strenuous Life*; more than mere taxidermy (a skill he learned as a child) or cattle ranching. He was speaking of imperialism, "righteous war," responsibility to self as well as to homeland. He was talking about individuals, families and nations. My version of the strenuous life is much less global and certainly less noble but definitely kinder to our animal friends. Kel and I call it cross-training.

When the work in the garden becomes tedious, repairing the fenceline gets tiring or digging holes to plant trees becomes hot and boring, either Kel or I will say, "It's good cross-training," in an attempt to motivate ourselves or the other. Carry two full 2-gallon watering cans down a steep hill and up another one and you are cross-training: alternately working the quadriceps and then the hamstrings and glutes, not to mention the workout your arms, shoulders and back are getting. Holding one end of the pipe (while your companion holds the other) that supports a thick, heavy roll of barbed wire while doing a walking lunge as you string the wire along each fence post? Cross-training with a partner. Wearing your knee-high rubber boots as you negotiate hillocks, gopher holes and cow patties works your

49

thighs and calves better than any late night infomercial contraption, and except for the cost of the boots, it's free. And it works. What about pushing and prodding square bales of hay, soggy with rain, and lifting them onto the back of a trailer? Excellent cross-training opportunity. Maybe you're the one shoveling that "mature" horse manure into 5-gallon buckets or maybe you're the one lifting, carrying and dumping those same buckets into the garden beds. No matter; either way you are getting some serious cross-training. I like to think that Teddy would approve.

Every activity that doesn't happen behind a desk and in front of a computer, that has me moving or using my muscles is an opportunity to challenge my stamina and fitness in different ways. I wouldn't trade the dirty, fatiguing chores I do out here for one minute at an office job. I'm not sure I could ever go back to one.

In my opinion, real life trumps fiction every time and T.R. is one of the more fascinating and inspiring characters in American history. There are lots of books about T. R. out there so hit the bookshelves. *The Strenuous Life* speech is an illuminating glimpse into Theodore Rex's era and yields, at least for me, some chilling advice for modern times.

- July 27, 2011

Purple Martins: If You Build It They Will Come

We were willing, open for business. Waiting. We followed the directions to the letter, positioning the gleaming white plastic "gourds" near the house and near water, yet with some trees nearby – but not *too* many trees, of course! Near open grassy areas – yet not near *too* much openness. The pole was set in cement and was of the telescoping kind so that we could be good landlords and check on the birds, clean the nests out at the end of the season. We read that we needed to provide string for their nests and crushed egg shells for their diet. We read that purple martins seek out people and even like to be chatted with so that they come to know their host's voice.

Two summers ago a flock of eight young purple martins hung around the property for about a week. They sat side by side on the electric wire above the garden and practiced their flying and then they'd preen. They spent the day zooming around the garden catching insects. We thought it was a good sign and felt sure that next spring some of these same birds would return to take up residence in the spotlessly clean and inviting purple martin complex near the pond. How could they not?

We never saw them again after that week. Then this spring a pair spent about half an hour carefully and thoroughly investigating each gourd. Again our hopes were raised and then quickly dashed as the picky couple flew off never to return.

There are all kinds of things you can do wrong when trying to lure purple martins to your area and sometimes it doesn't matter if you do everything right. It's a delicate balance of human involvement, timing and location. It's a little like it must've been for a gentleman to court a proper southern belle before the Civil War.

Weird thing is, even the sparrows, grackles, cow birds, wrens and bluebirds show no interest in the houses. Crows broke off the perches on some of them to be used in a manner only a crow would understand. All around town there are purple martin houses, most of them faded, falling apart, tipping over, and all of them are bursting at the seams with chatty martins. Or so it seems that way to us. Humbug.

Yet, we are still open, willing and waiting. The purple martin condo will remain as long as we live here. Sure, the white gourds are a painful reminder of our failure. They stand empty like half-built homes abandoned during the housing bust, forlorn and sad. But you never know. After the pole begins to cant, when the gourds fade and crack and acquire some patina and character we may yet get our birds.

- July 28, 2011

On Summer Days & Nights Circa 1976

Even as I wish for this summer's rapid demise, I cling to the days, oppressive as they are, reluctant for early sunsets and cold winds. I am not a fan of winter. But I've noticed that over time the flavor of summer has changed and I enjoy it less. Maybe it's the unbroken string of heat, maybe it's the weight of adult responsibilities, but the spell of summer is cracked, if not broken.

1976. The price of gas was .59-cents per gallon. Apple Computer Company was formed. America was celebrating its 200th birthday. Paul McCartney was singing silly love songs and Jimmy Carter defeated Gerald Ford to become the 39th President of the United States. I remember the bicentennial and Jimmy Carter (dad kept an unopened can of *Billy Beer* for many years) and at the tender age of 10 I was a Beatles and Paul McCartney fan. The other things were not even blips on my child radar. The most important event of that and every other year was the last day of school. The opening day of summer was field day, when there were games on the playground, a special boxed lunch, ice cream and last moments with friends we wouldn't see again until after Labor Day. At the end of this exuberant day, signing yearbooks and a final bus ride, I experienced a child's fleeting sadness that was quickly replaced by the anticipation of long summer days spent without textbooks (but with lots of books to read), bells ringing and raised hands, the pepperminty smell of the janitor's mop, hall passes and Miss Rossi telling me to pay attention.

During the days my siblings and I would be lost to the outdoors. I would roam the four hills - hogsbacks, as they were known - behind our house, dodging branches, mucking through the stream that trickled at the base of the hills searching for shell fossils and thick broken bits of colorful-glass or pottery. To cool down I'd spend some time poking through the dark corners of the old barn where the smell of horses, long since gone, still lingered. Rabbit cages stood empty and dusty, discarded furniture was stacked in precarious piles festooned with cobwebs. Most days the four of us siblings would troop the mile of dirt road to the swimming pool, towels wrapped around our heads to keep off the deer flies that hungrily circled us throughout the journey. In the morning we'd start out all energy and anticipation; in the evening we'd trudge home, lungs aching with pool water and stomachs empty. At least it was downhill most of the way. We were brown as fall leaves.

Ohio has great, banging summer storms and heavy rain provided entertainment, too. We'd get the okay from mom and head outside to stand in the downpour and wade into the water that collected in the depressions in the yard, the submerged grass swaying like seaweed. The air was warm, the drops of rain cool and thick. Lightning meant we had to come in until the sun broke through the thunderheads and the storm passed.

After dinner and while the light was still bright and yellow, we'd be back outside, riding bikes, playing with the dog or doing cartwheels and somersaults in the lawn beside the house. Reluctant to go back inside, my brothers and sister would sometimes play "ghost in the graveyard," and I could hear them moving around the yard, searching under bushes or behind trees. I was too afraid to join in, but I'd sit on the wooden stoop and sometimes give a hint as to the ghost's hiding place.

As the woods I played in all day yielded to night and became the domain of nocturnal creatures, the outdoors shrank to the small circle of light thrown by the lamp by the back door. Raccoons appeared in the circle, pawing into the dirt of a flower bed, dipping paws into puddles of water. Night was noisier than day: crickets, the pulsing hum of peepers, the guttural bursts from bullfrogs in the bog behind the hills, strange rustling sounds among the dried leaves. A heavy, earthy moistness hung in the air. Finally, worn out, we climbed the stairs to our beds. The old wooden sashes would be wide open and a gently thumping fan worked hard to pull in any hint of coolness. I never had to wait long for sleep to come.

Waking in the mornings to bright sunshine filtering through white curtains and the sound of the wooden stairs creaking as someone thumped downstairs to breakfast. The dog lay at the bottom of the steps, waiting for her playmates to get up. A summer day starting all over again in a seemingly endless procession. Freedom, green grass, tall trees, warmth, carelessness, the promise of a day left unplanned. The spell of summer circa 1976.

For more trivia on the year 1976 - or any other year - check out The People History.

- July 31, 2011

AUGUST

Wild In The City

At the forgotten edge of a run-down neighborhood in a well-known city in the Pacific Northwest, down a road that curves like a paperclip and is sheltered and shaded on both sides by soaring pines and thick-trunked hardwoods lies 35 acres of a taste of the wilderness. The sounds of the city slowly fade away on the walk down the black road. At the bottom of the hill one is cut off from the feel of civilization even though a busy road, high and away from sight, is not far, "as the crow flies."

Here there be monsters. Or, well, it's not impossible to imagine there are chimpanzees that will shortly commence screeching to one another as they swing from branch to branch. Large birds with big bobbing heads, thick, clacking beaks and garishly-colored feathers might call out, warning their kin to the presence of humans invading their kingdom. Boa constrictors could well be *at this exact moment* sliding, slithering down the pebbled bark of a tulip poplar, coming to see what all of the fuss is about. They are all just out of sight, at the peripheral edges of vision.

From deep down in the dark green comes the bright sound of water. Fallen logs, crumbling with rot and scarred with the erratic paths of chewing insects obscure a stream that bisects the forest. Legend says that once, long ago, a horse lived in here and died, alone, beside the stream.

Among the ferns that grow nearly to shoulder height there are things (probably!) that crawl and scurry and sting. Strung up between the trees, beautifully spun but deadly webs sway and glitter in the weak sunlight that penetrates through the leaves and the brambled undergrowth. There is a path and it would be wise to stay true to it.

The terminus of the journey through this tiny slice of forest comes at the brief and tantalizing view of the stream which tumbles over slick brown rocks and is squishy at the edges with shiny mud. One gazes longingly at the other side - a shortcut out - that is as green and wild as what lays behind yet offers a glimpse of the city houses just ahead.

There is no escape from here, though. One must turn back and retrace their steps through the jungle.

- August 22, 2016

Romancing the Mower

It starts around 7:30 pm not long after the dinner dishes have been washed. When the west-facing bricks still radiate from the heat of the day, but after the sun has melted into the treeline and the night jars call to one another from the deep shadows of the woods. Over at the neighbor's in the unseen distance there is the sound of a lawnmower starting up, a wavering drone, followed by another from farther off, and then my mower roaring to life. I'm covered head to toe: baseball cap, thick gloves, sunglasses, ear muffs, long-sleeved shirt, pants, and boots. This is serious work.

I come from a short but proud line of females who love to mow. My aunt and my mother and I all find it satisfying. Therapeutic. Alone with our scattered and random thoughts. Time to work out a nagging problem, the emptiness to play out long lost or in-progress dreams. The sound of the engine, muffled by hearing protection, lulls and calms. The handlebar vibrates soothingly. Tomorrow there may be a blister or two, a development that brings great satisfaction. Maybe we just like to see the evidence of work being done. Ahead of us is an unkempt plot of tangled Bermuda, dandelion, Johnson, crabgrass, and clover. Behind us lies a close shave, smooth and tidy as a putting green.

It's been this way since the birth of suburbia. As summer twilights creep across both postage-stamp-sized lawns and rolling hilled estates, good, hard-working folks change out of their respectable clothes, heft ungainly red cans of gasoline that bang against knees. They unscrew the dipstick and check the oil with a dirty Kleenex found buried deep in a pocket. They prime and pull and pull again and the engine sputters and catches. The tops of shoes turn green, and moist, torn fragments of grass cling to pant legs. A grasshopper hitches a ride on a hat brim. Soon it is too dark to see what has been cut and what hasn't, but we press on until every square inch is tamed and sheared.

One by one the engines go silent like voices leaving the chorus. The day shutters down completely and the crickets begin to rev *their* motors. Inside, the oily stink of fossil fuel lingers in nostrils hours later, but open windows let in the cool green smell of grass. The sense of satisfaction, of work well done, of sweating, and toiling, and improving, even if the neatness lasts only a few days. Keeping up with the neighbors, pride of ownership, taming nature. Mediation, problem solving, novel-writing. It's all there in the simple act of mowing the lawn.

- August 20, 2013

Taking the Salt Air

Just off of I-80 – the side that heads towards the town of Wendover (which spills over into Nevada) – and onto Reno (more than 500 long miles down the road), along the crusty, stinking banks of the Great Salt Lake, sits the Saltair Pavilion. A curiosity, an updated relic from another age. First built in 1893 as a resort and family-oriented amusement park, the building burned down in 1925. It was rebuilt only to go up in flames once again in 1931. It wasn't until fifty years later that someone undertook to recreate the resort on the apparently doomed site. This time it wasn't fire but water that plagued the new Saltair. The Great Salt Lake rose and flooded the building.

It's nice and dry now and is a functioning party and concert venue, but it retains an air of neglect. The latest building is loosely modeled on the ornate original, but the tarnished onion domes, dull adobe facade and pointed arches are a Las Vegas architect's perversion of a Russian Orthodox church crossed with the Topkapi Palace in Istanbul. Swallows' nests crowd the ledges along the top of the building, windows are stained by the heavy salt air and bird droppings. A handwritten sign taped to a side door window admonishes, *The Building is Closed No Bathrooms No Sightseeing No Trespassing Don't Ask!!* But what's in a sign? When we were there it didn't stop several people from trying to open the chained and locked door.

- August 6, 2012

Cloudbusting

You're like my yo-yo
That glowed in the dark
What made it special
Made it dangerous
So I bury it
And forget

- Kate Bush, *Cloudbusting*

July has slipped into August and the blue sky, usually so welcome, has become a reproach. We are being deprived of rain and I miss it. Every living thing here misses it. I get a little desperate, eyeing the perfect, puffy white clouds that now and again linger overhead, somehow neither providing rain nor sheltering us from the heat of the sun. Thoughts turn to cloud seeding, rain-dancing, cloudbusting.

Years ago while living in Cambridge, MA, I became interested in Wilhelm Reich, solely because of a song by Kate Bush called *Cloudbusting*. The song is from the point of view of Reich's son, Peter, and there's quite a lot of information about Reich packed into that 5:08 song. I found the book that inspired Kate shelved on one of the dark basement stacks of Widener Library at Harvard, rarely checked out, all but forgotten.

Reich was an Austrian psychoanalyst, psychiatrist and scientist who emigrated to the United States in 1939. He practiced some controversial methods involving touch therapy and having his patients strip down to their underwear during sessions (it gets more interesting than that, but let's keep it G-rated). Reich was big into something he called orgone – a cosmic energy – that he believed was responsible for everything from the formation of galaxies and cancer cells to the biological expressions of sexuality. Powerful stuff. This belief led to the invention of the orgone accumulator. He built some large enough for his patients to sit inside. But he also invented something called a Cloudbuster, a machine that he claimed could form clouds out of blue sky and make them release rain. The Cloudbuster was believed by Maine farmers to be responsible for saving their 1953 blueberry crop from a potentially devastating drought.

Fortunes started to take a downward turn for Reich in the late 1940s when the FDA took a closer look at his practice – in particular the orgone accumulator. Kate Bush sings of black cars coming for Reich and a radioactive yo-yo buried in the ground. In real life, he was accused of violating an FDA injunction and his books and papers were burned and the orgone accumulators destroyed. He died in prison in 1957 only a few days prior to his release.

I don't have a brain built for psychiatry or meteorology, let alone the esoteric study of orgonomy, but I wouldn't mind Dr. Reich paying a visit to Oklahoma, climbing up behind the wheel of his Cloudbuster and pulling some rain from the blue skies.

Wilhelm Reich is a one-of-a-kind character from history. Seriously, you can't make this stuff up! For a very personal perspective, read Peter Reich's book, *A Book of Dreams*. Meanwhile, the video for *Cloudbusting* is vintage Kate Bush kookiness with Kate playing the part of Peter and Donald Sutherland as Wilhelm.

- August 1, 2011

The Loneliness of a Single Shoe on the Highway

I can understand the bunched-up article of clothing, the broken Styrofoam cooler, the beat up mattress or recliner, even the battered microwave. Fast food bags, cups, beer bottles, cardboard and tires are no-brainers. But it's the appearance of a lone shoe that gets me thinking. Small and forlorn, holding the personal, intimate shape of a human foot, it's almost a living thing as it rests on the concrete. Cars and vans, trucks and motorcycles speed by, the people inside mostly oblivious to it.

It's surprising how often one sees a single sneaker, pump, work boot or sandal resting along the highway. Was it thrown out of the window in anger? Drunken abandon? Did it somehow come loose from luggage tied to the top of a car and tumble onto the roadway? Sometimes the shoe is positioned so it looks as if at any moment it will begin striding purposefully forward. Other times it lies on its side, exhausted with the sadness of its fate, empty of hope. I imagine someone walking along with one shoe, loping unevenly up and down, up and down, somehow unaware of their shoeless foot until the forgotten companion is too many miles behind to retrieve.

It's a lonely image, the abandoned shoe. Rocked by passing semis, drenched with rain and snow, coated with road dirt and salt, it sits stoically through it all, waiting to be rescued. *If I just stay right here, my owner will come and get me!* Does the owner miss it? Do they wonder as to the whereabouts of the companion to the shoe they still have, puzzling as they hold the remaining one? It's like breaking the bond between twins.

And of the shoe still in its owner's possession? What is its worth? Whether right or left, its utility is stripped away, the task it was made for unfulfilled. Yet there it is, perfectly good. Sturdy or stylish and/or beloved, it makes no difference. Its destiny is the trash can while its mate waits patiently along the side of the road.

- August 4, 2011

Go ahead and Google "lone shoe on highway" and see what you find. Lots. There's even a Wikipedia entry on it!

The Sugar House

At the end of Heath Road was a 40-or-so acre property that, though as a child it wouldn't have occurred to me, was a wormhole between the agrarian, self-sufficient past and the city-dwelling, import-dependent future. An old couple lived there, here I'll call them the Van Aken's. The Van Aken's land was a perfect mix of field and forest. They had black-and-white dairy cows that browsed the pastures and fought the pull of gravity as they grazed along the steep, rocky slope that led down to a thin stream. When we moved in mom asked the Van Akens to our housewarming party and they declined since the party was right at milking time.

In the summer, Mr. Van Aken grew corn on the fields that dipped up and down like deep sea waves. A neat but tired white-washed country home sat partially hidden by tall evergreens and behind it sat a sturdy red barn that dwarfed the house. Somewhere deep in the hardwood forest behind the barn sat a maple sugar house. Except for the high power lines that crossed the property, the corner on which the Van Aken's land sat was a piece of early 20th century life.

Ohio is paradise for big trees. It's the amount of moisture, I guess, but the maples, oaks and beeches grow massive trunks and their branches spread out, touching their neighbors' branches, providing a vast, green, shady canopy for the undergrowth below. Mr. Van Aken had metal buckets on all of the big sugar maples on his property and come early spring it was time to harvest the sap and boil it down.

Vermont gets most of the maple syrup attention in the U.S., but northeastern Ohio is no syrup slouch. Down the road from the Van Aken's is a small town that has some of the richest maple syrup around and it's harvested and sold there. I love it so much I order it to be shipped to me in Oklahoma.

One winter Mr. Van Aken invited us kids to come into the sugar house and watch while he boiled down the syrup. We made the journey to the house on a wagon led by a couple of his horses. It hardly seems possible, but it's true. The smell of woodsmoke met us before we even came up upon the cabin – rich and thick. Gray-white clouds of smoke drifted up through the trees. Once inside the house the heavy, sweet smell of maple surrounded us and we watched the amber syrup bubble in large vats. It was hot in the cabin, the fragrance and warmth nearly overwhelming us. Mrs. Van Aken was there, wearing her bonnet, stirring the syrup with a long stick.

After the elder Van Akens died, the developers came sniffing around the idyllic land. They'd already eaten up vast acres of open fields along our road. The corner lot and all of that land were ideal for cookie-cutter suburban homes built too close together. For a couple of years we worried that one day we'd see bulldozers knocking down the beautiful old trees and leveling the fields. But the Van Aken's daughter has held on to the property somehow and now it sits quiet and unused, the old house gone. Otherwise the past lives on undisturbed. Grass grows tall in the former corn rows with no dairy cows or tractors to keep the fields shorn. The sugar maples go untapped. I wonder if the dull silver buckets still hang from the trees and if the old sugar house still stands.

- August 5, 2011

In the Stacks

Early in the morning I'd let myself into the building, turn on the computer and take the stuffy elevator down to the stacks. It was always a few degrees warmer down there with a faint and comforting ticking noise coming from the furnace. I had the whole building to myself for two hours before I had to head to my full-time job. The first floor room I worked in was a soft gray in the winter morning light, the desks, bookcases, trash cans and chairs motionless, immovable as mountains, frozen in their abandoned positions. They could have been that way for centuries.

Nobody was really certain as to what was down there in the basement, book-wise. My job was to catalog what was, to dust off the old and forgotten and reunite them with their cataloged mates.

I'd turn lights on as I went along the stacks and since they were on timers, they'd eventually click off slowly one by one. The ceiling was low and off at the edges of the room were darker rectangles, gaping doorways into areas I had no curiosity to explore. I avoided looking up into the inky depths of the ceiling. Spiders. And things.

I'd load up a cart with about ten books, choosing from an area I'd cataloged the day before, working my way through decades of old city and county records. Then I'd take the elevator back to the first floor. My goodness these were dull books. Except sometimes for the photographs which offered intriguing glimpses into the past. The accomplishments of towns and cities: bridges built and tunnels dug; waterworks and welfare rolls, taxes collected. Endless numbers and figures, maps, charts and graphs. There's something poignant about our diligence in keeping such records only to see the once-relevant data end up in anonymous row upon row of mouldering books on shelves in a dark basement.

In most cases I am a person not afraid of letting go of material things. Too much stuff makes me feel weighted down and anxious. But I hold on to some things and I wonder about my tendency to keep old lists and journals filled with scribbled thoughts and ideas, the mostly dull facts and figures of my own existence. Letters and numbers out of context, lacking detail, body or explanation. Is it some need to leave a record of my intentions and accomplishments for after I'm gone, minor as they may be? Do I feel a need to prove to future generations that I had goals, that getting things done was important to me? The dry bread crumbs of personal data leading back to someone long gone from a world that is only about the present

- August 8, 2011

Where the Outside Meets the Inside

We try hard to defend the boundaries set by the brick walls of the house. To me it's very clear where the outside belongs and where my indoor sanctuary begins. Yet the four-, six- and eight-legged creatures pass through freely with neither respect nor awareness of our barriers. No brushing off their feet on the welcome mat or a quick *anyone home?* before coming inside.

They find their way in despite the screens, storm sashes and doors. We've scooped up or chased out hummingbirds, wrens (they love to build their nests in boots), slate-colored skinks, mice, snakes, frogs, scorpions of all sizes, grasshoppers and crickets, of course, wasps and sleek salamanders decorated with electric blue stripes. Pill bugs appear inside in droves just before it rains. There is no end to the spiders that move easily in and out, especially beige-toned wolf spiders.

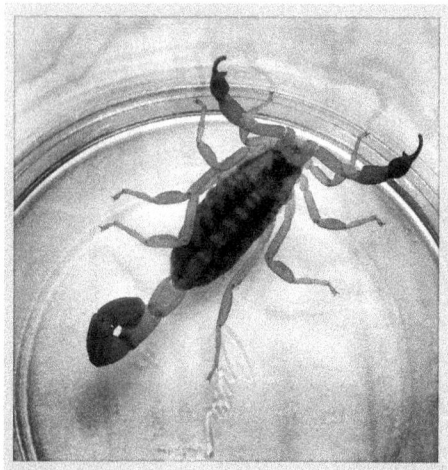

All spiders seem to adore the dusty corners at the bottom of the doors and once we found a fat Black Widow snug in her cottony web in a spot our feet brush past countless times every day. Don't get me started on the Brown Recluse spiders that apparently think the house was constructed as their personal hunting ground and shelter. I've never, ever seen one outdoors.

Tiny spiders, crab-like and one shade lighter than their host's green leaves make the journey indoors aboard the

bunch of basil I've just cut. Leafhoppers, ants and small bee-
tles catch rides on hat brims for a crow's nest vantage point.

This is one advantage of winter. The creatures go where
they should – either to warmer climes, to their maker or
into some safe, dark place to wait out the cold. A place
where I cannot see them. If I can't see them, they don't exist. Even the Brown Recluses have the decency to disappear
for a few months and call a halt to their nightly patrol of the
baseboards.

- August 10, 2011

No Life Jackets Allowed: Glen & Bessie Hyde Run the Grand Canyon

My own experience of the Grand Canyon has been so brief as to really not count at all. During an ill-conceived move to California back in the early 90s, I picked up a friend in Fort Collins, CO on my way west. He'd been participating in an Ultimate Frisbee tournament and needed a ride back to San Francisco, my destination. We decided it was a good opportunity to do some sightseeing along the way so we stopped at various places all deserving of weeks of our time rather than hours, but such is youth. Zion, Bryce Canyon and Las Vegas all got cursory visits, but our stop at the Grand Canyon was the briefest. We arrived at dark and spent the night in a cabin and the next morning headed over to the South Rim, walked a little bit, peered over the side and snapped some photos before eating breakfast and continuing on our way to the Golden State. I'm almost ashamed to call myself an American.

I got no closer on a recent trip from Utah back to Oklahoma (taking the very southerly route to avoid bad weather), but did pick up an interesting book about the Grand Canyon at The Little America hotel in Flagstaff, AZ. An aside: I love The Little America. Tall pine trees surround the hotel and obscure the view of the highway. The room decor is pure 1970s, but spotless and very comfortable. Giant logs in a huge stone fireplace pop and snap as the flames warm the lobby. The gift shop sells fringed leather coats, cowboy boots and chunky turquoise jewelry. They also sell books about regional topics and I picked up one titled, *Over the Edge: Death in Grand Canyon,* by Michael Ghiglieri & Thomas Myers. A true page-turner. I can't resist books whose topics are death: coroners' memoirs, stories from the Body Farm, true murder mysteries. You get the idea. *Death in Grand Canyon* goes into exhaustive detail about the ways and hows of every known fatality in the park. Exhaustive as in an inventory of names, dates and the sordid details. But it's more than dry lists. The narrative is fascinating and entertaining.

There are, let's call them, the run-of-the-mill mishaps – people slipping into the abyss, people playing practical jokes that go horribly wrong, suicides, rafting accidents, heat- and thirst-related deaths, distance misjudgments and the occasional murder. There are the characters you may already know something about: John Wesley Powell who navigated the Green and Colorado Rivers (three of his men were murdered after they left the expedition), The Kolb Brothers, skilled river-runners and photographers who filmed their journeys down the Green and Colorado Rivers; the fugitive, Danny Ray Horning, a convicted bank robber, child molester and murderer who had escaped from prison and went on the lam for 54 days in 1992 (complete with kidnappings, thefts, shoot-outs and car chases. Coincidentally, Horning trawled for kidnap victims at the above-mentioned Little America hotel.). Yipes.

One story that caught my imagination was about Bessie Haley and Glen Rollin Hyde. Back in 1927 Bessie was a 21-year old divorcee from West Virginia who'd moved to San Francisco for a fresh start and to study at an arts academy. Apparently not content, she and her roommate bought one way tickets on a ship bound for Los Angeles. The roommate had plans to make it big in Hollywood and Bessie went along for the adventure. Bessie apparently was prone to going along for adventures. During the trip, Bessie met Glen and the sparks flew. They became inseparable and Bessie's roommate sought her fortune in L.A. alone.

Glen was from Idaho and with a few river runs under his belt nursed a dream of running the Colorado River through the Grand Canyon – with Bessie – making them the first couple to do it and her the first woman to complete the journey. If they made it. The two married and fleshed out their dream. The run, they figured, would make them famous and they imagined touring the country giving lectures about their adventures, the money and fame rolling in. To make it even more interesting, they planned on making the run in a scow that Glen built, setting speed records for traversing the canyons AND doing it all without life jackets.

I think you can probably see where this is going. Glen's boat was a sorry mess. A Green River local pronounced the scow "a floating coffin." But they set off anyway. Struggling through Cataract Canyon, Bessie was ejected from the boat but was rescued by Glen. At Lee's Ferry, an experienced boatman advised them to wear life vests. Glen declined.

Farther down the river, Glen was the one ejected from the boat, but with Bessie's help, he was able to pull himself back in. In late November 1928, the pair made it to Phantom Ranch and resupplied, once again being urged (this time by veteran Grand Canyon boatman Emery Kolb) to use life jackets. Glen replied that they didn't need no stinkin' artificial aids. Bessie by this time had had enough, but was unable to pull herself away from Glen.

Turns out it wasn't the scow's fault. On December 6, Glen's father, Rollin, waited at Needles to pick up Glen and Bessie. Ten days later he was still waiting. On Christmas Eve, searchers (including the Kolb brothers) found the Hyde's boat, intact, caught in an eddy at Mile 237 – still loaded with all of the Hyde's possessions, even Bessie's purse. A campsite was found miles upstream from the boat, but further searches around the area revealed no other indication that the Hydes had been there. It was speculated that a particularly difficult set of rapids catapulted the Hydes into the river where they drowned near Mile 232. The boat continued on without them and then became caught in some rocks.

Like the best legends, this story remains an unsolved mystery. Glen and Bessie's bodies were never found. Some suggested that the Hydes had been murdered. Over the years rumors and questions persisted. In 1971 a gray-haired lady on a Grand Canyon rafting tour confessed to her fellow passengers that she was Bessie Hyde and that she'd murdered Glen to escape his abuse. She later recanted. It was also rumored that rafter Georgie White Clark was really Bessie Hyde. Documents found among her possessions hinted at a connection. Neither the gray-haired lady confessing to murder nor Ms. Clark bore a resemblance to Bessie, though, and the rumors remained just that.

One thing is for sure, however. Bessie did become the first woman to run the river – at least until Mile 232.

- August 11, 2011

Driving Into Rain

Up ahead the blue-gray bulk of storm clouds shades the line of trees to a glowing, bright green, a trick of light played on the eye. Above, the sky is mostly blue and sunlit. Thick beams of light stream through more benevolent clouds than those in the distance. The concrete of the road is still dry. A few fat drops of rain hit the windshield like thick oil, streaking through the layer of dust you hadn't noticed before. The rain picks up suddenly and the light shifts, changes, darkens. Wind buffets the car.

Suddenly the rain comes, falling straight down and heavy, bouncing up off of the road, turning it black and shiny. The inside of the car is a comforting sanctuary despite the staccato of the rain on the roof, isolating you from the wet and the wind. Nevertheless you grip the wheel a little tighter and lean closer to the windshield. The sound of the radio becomes a distraction and you turn it off. Car lights on the other side of the road shoot long, bright fuzzy beams onto the pavement while cars in front drag red wavy lines behind them. You are pulled along by their crimson threads, heading deeper into the gray, driving straight into the storm.

- August 13, 2011

Bones and Shells

It was a day for finding bones and shells. We walked along the broken fence line, heading towards the tumble of rocks to the north. The long streaky shadows of morning lay across the humps of thick grass, a deep orange sun beginning to tip the treetops in yellow. I called to Ike, who was lagging, and he ran up to me, lifting his head with the weight of his prize – proudly carrying a turtle's shell he'd unearthed from its resting place. A box turtle. The occupant was long gone. Small, pure white bones rattled around the inside of the shell. Pieces of the thin, translucent veneer of the shell, shiny and fragile as mica, were peeling off. Ike left his prize behind with the strain of climbing the rocks.

Later, up in the western pasture along the edge of the woods, we found the bones of a small coyote, the tail still thick with soft fur, everything else clean and white. The bones lay as if the pup had rolled over onto its back in a posture of complete abandon, of feeling safe.

We continued across the western pasture and along the road, down past the derelict horsehead pump and then towards the pond that is slowly drying up and disappearing in the drought. A green heron took flight as we approached. We walked gingerly onto the cracking mud, the shoreline wider now and gooey in spots, like fudge. Walking on earth recently covered in water, walking on a small scale natural disaster. A cow's skull, hip bones and leg bones dyed a deep orange from their time submerged, lay stuck in the mud. With rain the relics will disappear again under water and rest, safe from our dispassionate scrutiny. Ike and I looked more closely at the mud. Tiny shells, swirls of white and pink, freckled the deep brown clay.

Back up along the line of trees, this time along the eastern edge, another coyote tragedy. The bones small as those of a cat, lying in a sad heap, picked over, tossed about. Another restless coyote soul trotting over the prairie.

Nature holds no secrets. She is blunt and honest and harsh and sweet. The living and the dead, side by side, bones unburied and shells abandoned – all to be reclaimed by the earth, nurturing the next generations. As for Ike and me, we can only hope to fulfill such a noble destiny. In the meantime, we will explore and run, sniff, play and wonder and pay our respects to the white bones and the empty shells.

- August 15, 2011

A Town Called I.X.L.

There is no easy way for us to get to Tulsa. One must ride the curves, behind the slow cars and through the school zones and small towns with their speed traps and along the ups and the downs of the two-lanes that lead, just past Bristow, to the turnpike. $1.25, please. From there it's a straight shot, but much less interesting.

It's not a bad thing, driving this way. How else would one find a town called I.X.L. (population 59, at last count)? Heading north into I.X.L. the sign says: I.X.L. Returning south it says: IXL. To the south of I.X.L. is a pecan grove with acres of tall and wide trees. Underneath the trees the grass is smooth and green as a lawn. Cows drowse and graze in the cool and peaceful shadows. The North Canadian River crosses one's path on the way to I.X.L. It's a shallow but wide river, with sand bars dividing it nearly in two. This year it's especially low, but the white egrets and herons still come to saunter along the sandy banks and fish.

If there were an easy way to go to Tulsa, you'd miss seeing towns called Newby, Gypsy, Castle, Iron Post and Welty. You'd miss the countless small churches along the way: the Welty Full Gospel, the Gypsy Holiness Church, the African Methodist Episcopal, the Welcome Bell Chapel and the Goodwill Baptist, some so far off the road that all you see is a faded and peeling sign pointing down a dry and dusty road.

It would be a shame not to add to one's knowledge the various offerings from these towns: Clark's Maintenance, Hoss' Tire Shop (with the colorfully-painted stone wall), Rob's Magneto Service, and the Speed-a-Way right on the corner. You never know when you might find yourself in need of their services. "Tiger" is running for Head Chief this year and would appreciate your vote. In Bristow you can buy yourself a brand new Ford, load up on barbed wire, eat a pizza, visit the archery store or simply stop in at the gas station for "hot subs, cold beer, cheap cig." If your old VW Beetle or Rabbit needs a part, look no further than the VW graveyard with its long lines of rusty, windowless bugs. Your dune buggy needs can also be met. And the Paden Mud Bog would be glad to get your business, if one could figure out exactly what the Paden Mud Bog was selling.

- August 17, 2011

One Side of a Conversation

Have you got yer turnips in yet and yer mustard greens? Time to get those in. I love me some turnips. And them mustard greens. Get those in for the fall. Now how do you cook 'em? Uh huh. Uh huh. Yeah? Hmm. Why, I just boil 'em up real good, get some butter on there, lotsa salt and pepper. Eat a whole plate of those. Do you put yours up? You can put 'em up, yep. Just boil 'em real good and put 'em in the freezer – like yer spinach. Same thing. Have 'em all year. But you better get those in the ground.

No, ain't nobody got good tomatoes this year. No, sir. Not even Bill Yoder out there on 48. Plants tall as you. But they was just burnin' up. Couldn't water 'em enough. Gave up and dug 'em in. And the watermelons. Damnedest thing. He had a whole field of 'em. In two days them hogs ate ever' single one of them melons. All that was left was rind. Cleaned right out. Saw it with my own eyes. Nothing like the pork barbeque, though. Too bad y'all are veg'tarian cuz my boy he does the barbeque. Put him up against anyone on that.

Well, I don't have much of a sweet tooth. No. Not really. But yer pies and yer cookies – can't beat a good fruit pie, no sir. Not the cakes. I can do without the frosting. People put too much frosting on there and it gets so you can't taste the cake! But a good fruit pie. Hard to beat that. What's that? Uh huh. Well, yep, that's good, sure, but me I like the rhubarb. You got rhubarb in the garden? You should get you some rhubarb. Puts up good, too. Hey, are those apples of yours ready yet? Let me know when them apples are ready.

I love me some beans. T'other night I had a mess of white beans, now, normally I don't really like the white beans but these were darn good. Now you give me some of them red beans – wooo! – I could eat my way out of a wash tub

of them red beans! Did you plant beans this year? Alrighty
now. Uh huh. Get yer turnips and yer mustard greens in
– you can eat the turnip greens, too. Better get them in,
though.

- August 19, 2011

A Tall Grayish Figure (Part I)

That morning I'd run my usual route up the hill to R, down to P, across the bridge and through the neighborhoods of Dupont Circle working my way to M Street. I ran along silent and empty M into Georgetown where it was only me and the water truck that was showering the large baskets of pink petunias hanging from the lamp posts. I turned left and followed 29th, enjoying the ease of the downhill, until I came to the canal and turned right to follow the narrow green path alongside it, past a homeless man sleeping on a bench, then under the huge mulberry tree which drops its dark purple fruit into the water below where the turtles snap them up like sweet, juicy bugs.

I got to the place where the old brick buildings tower overhead and cling to the high edge of the tall stone wall. To my left the water was a dark green, unmoving. Up ahead I could see something on the path, a tall grayish figure. I hesitated, aware that there were no stone steps out, no escape route back up into the city. And the path was very narrow. I wondered how deep the canal was and once in would I be able to pull myself up over the other side. My legs kept moving forward, though. Once running I'm reluctant to stop for fear I won't start again. The figure grew larger.

To my relief, the ill-defined shape formed itself not into threatening man but into bird. A huge bird. A Great Blue Heron peering down into the canal. I slowed then so as not to startle the bird. I assumed he would take flight immediately anyway, but he didn't, even as I came within a few feet of him. He was as tall as I, standing at the edge with a lonely and contemplative dignity, attired in soft grays and whites and embellished with wisps of delicate, long feathers. A figure from Colonial America. What did he see in the depths besides breakfast? He seemed not to notice me as I admired him and then walked past him to continue my run.

A few weeks later I was again running along the canal path, this time in the opposite direction to where the canal slips away and curves off towards the Potomac. It was a bright Sunday morning. Again the city was still and quiet. At the bend in the canal the tall gray figure stood, his slim face and long yellow beak turned towards the sun, wings spread wide to absorb the warmth. His eyes were closed – at least that is the way I remember it. I slowed and then stopped to watch him for a few minutes, wondering what a heron thinks: ancient memories passed down through heron generations of swamps brimming with frogs and quiet ponds jumping with unwary fish; unhurried flights over lush green landscapes, or maybe of empty and lonely places that have never known the taint of man.

- August 21, 2011

Pictures From A Trip

I keep thinking of him as just being on a trip. He was always somewhere else. Toronto, Chicago, hitchhiking to Alaska. So to me, right now, Mark is simply away. On the road. Doing a job somewhere on the other side of the globe. I'm waiting for the late night when I get a call. I'll pick up the phone and hear the long-distance hum. It will be a collect call from Mark. He will speak first. "Hello, sweet. I love you." And I will answer, "The charge is reversible."

- from Pictures From A Trip, by Tim Rumsey

My mother gave me the book after she'd read it. It was around the same time that we were deep into Edward Abbey, especially *Desert Solitaire* and *The Monkey Wrench Gang*. With a little convincing we would've taken up chain saws to slay a few billboards and filled the gas tanks of a bulldozer or two with Karo syrup and sand.

This book, *Pictures From A Trip*, was completely different, yet with a shared spirit. It's about a road trip; a certain time in one's life, after college but before the weight of real responsibilities ties one to place and routine. The ending is given away in the prologue, but when you get to those last pages, it still hits you like a sucker punch to the stomach. It's a joyful, funny book. It's also one of the saddest books I've ever read.

I've kept a copy of the book through my various wanderings and it has yellowed around the edges. I recently reread it. It's held up well. It meant something to me back when I first read it but it resonates with me now with a painful keenness. The narrator's brother could be my brother as a young man: free, impulsive, vibrant, careless, funny and sensitive. The brother's relationship to each other reminds me of a sisterly version of mine with my brother who over the years has been protector, role model, sounding board and confidante. When he moved to Utah for college I was heartbroken. When he got a job and excelled at it, I was proud.

85

I envied the ease of his physicality, a natural athleticism I lacked. I always thought he was the handsomest guy I knew. In short, I adored (and adore) my oldest brother. His friendship, love, humor, orneriness, goodness and guidance, I cherish. As the eldest, he forged the rough path upon which his siblings walked with relative ease. His independence is his hallmark, his soft side an oft-hidden, unpolished jewel. Now he lives with something for which I possess no real understanding, though when alone with my thoughts, I try. I struggle to make sense of what is happening to him, but I lack the right experiences. I can only work with the rudimentary tools that I have. Nevertheless, I understand enough to balk at the the story's ending.

In September we will meet in eastern Utah to run our third annual 10k together. It's a quiet and peaceful race. We have

long stretches of it to ourselves. The course winds through Buckhorn Wash and terminates at the San Rafael River under a large tent. We walk – sometimes run – on the red dust, near petroglyphs scraped casually into the stone walls that line the road and past thick stands of cottonwoods that choke the dry river bed. Ribbons of dusky color flow across the surface of skyscraper-high rocks and dark magenta stains drip towards the ground. Walking the dirt road, walking through and past eons. The sky blooms from pre-dawn black to robin's egg blue. In bright morning sunshine, we will sprint downhill for the finish line at the river, collect our medals and feel good.

Afterwards we plan on extending our road trip together, heading north to Wyoming to spend a few days with two good people and a friendship born of bad news, tentative hope and empathy. I'm looking forward to being on the road with my brother, talking, listening to music and to seeing our friends. I know that my brother will be impatient for home. Life has always moved at an accelerated speed for him, now especially so – and the Type A in me chafes at the time away from my home. But the sister in me pleads for more time with my brother, more miles on the road, more conversations and shared memories.

- August 24, 2011

The Wyoming portion of our trip didn't happen for reasons I now can't remember. Instead we drove west to Ely, Nevada and The Great Basin, then up to Wendover before returning to Utah. I wrote about that part of the trip in *Utah State Route 159*. You can find it in the *September* chapter of this book.

Night Spiders

The evening of the day I wrote my short tribute to the yellow and black garden orb, I settled into bed to continue reading *The Immense Journey: An Imaginative Naturalist Explores the Mysteries of Man and Nature* by Loren Eiseley and came across this:

> It was a cold autumn evening, and, standing under a suburban street light in a spate of leaves and beginning snow, I was suddenly conscious of some huge and hairy shadows dancing over the pavement. They seemed attached to an odd, globular shape that was magnified above me. There was no mistaking it. I was standing under the shadow of an orb-weaving spider...There she was, the universe running down around her, warmly arranged among her guy ropes attached to the lamp supports – a great black and yellow embodiment of the life force, not giving up to either frost or stepladders. She ignored me and went on tightening and improving her web.

The *exact* kind of spider - this one finding warmth on a cold autumn evening in the false sunlight of a streetlamp - to which I was paying homage. It amazes me how often these small coincidences happen.

As Mr. Eiseley sent my thoughts back to spiders and our missing black-and-yellow garden orbs, I ran a quick mental inventory of other insect companions and found that there are quite a few on the MIA list this summer. While there are more grasshoppers than usual, there are no mosquitoes (hooray!), no deer flies (though the irksome horseflies have survived), or fireflies; not a single ladybug or her less welcome imposter (the Asian Lady Beetle). We are missing yet another kind of orb-weaving spider. These I call the Night Spiders, because they begin their work as evening falls and they are gone again, or nearly gone by the time the sun rises. They can be fairly large. They're a light speckled-brown and tuck themselves into tiny, prickly balls and wait in the center of their perfectly-constructed webs. They populate the length of our tree-lined driveway, one after the other suspended in the branches, sending long strings of thick silk from one side to the other, sometimes anchoring their webs on rocks along the drive. Then they begin the slow and intricate task of spinning the deadly parts of their webs. In the morning they patiently reel in their hard work – I know because I've watched them – but occasionally they leave a strand or two. I know *this* because I've walked into them. It's like brushing past a remnant of the night world, something from the dark, something of which you catch only the smallest, unsettling glimpse.

Another small coincidence. The morning after I wrote this, I stepped outside into the pre-dawn gray and pink and there, right by the door, was a Night Spider, as if to say, *yes, we are still here, human*. She'd strung her web between the tall holly and a small bush growing up from the monkey grass. It was too dark to take a picture, so I waited about an hour and came back. By that time, there was no trace of her or her web.

- August 26, 2011

A Tall Grayish Figure (Part II)

The elegant gray figure has followed me here, or rather, there are many like him (or her) here in Oklahoma. They are far more reclusive than my Georgetown fellow. If they catch even a sniff of our presence they take flight.

We have one frequent visitor to the pond near our house. He glides in over the trees, drops low and working his wings, lands expertly along the edge of the water and resettles his feathers. After a few moments of reacquainting himself with his surroundings, he begins walking gingerly along the edge of the pond, his high, backward steps measured and slow. He looks like an old man walking contentedly through a park with his hands clasped behind his back. No rush, just passing the time, enjoying the view. But the heron is a hunter. His disinterested behavior only lulls the water creatures into a sense of safety. He studies the ground as if choosing among the offerings of tiny delicacies on a silver tray. The pond edge pops with mud-brown frogs no bigger than a thumbnail and small fish dart in and out of the shallows. He stops and stares hard into the water. Under the heron's laser gaze there surely is a frog or a fish that isn't paying attention.

One late afternoon as the setting sun lit the eastern side of the pond, a heron stood among the tall grasses at the pond's edge and gazed into the still brown water. Suddenly his head darted forward and we saw a large fish struggling in his beak. With quick and careful maneuverings, the heron twisted the fish so that it followed the line of his beak and bit by bit, the heron swallowed his prey. It looked to be too big for even this large bird and for several moments we watched as the heron gulped, the shape of the fish clearly visible within the long neck. I was reminded of Carson Mc-Culler's story about a jockey who was so small and thin one could see the outline of a lamb chop in his stomach after

90

he'd eaten it. The fish then was completely gone, down into the heron's stomach and he resumed his measured steps along the shore, surveying the delicacies below.

- August 31, 2011

The quote, from Carson McCuller's short story, *The Jockey*, is:

Sylvester turned to the rich man, 'If he eats a lamb chop, you can see the shape of it in his stomach a [sic] hour afterward. He can't sweat things out of him anymore. He's a hundred and twelve and a half. He's gained three pounds since we left Miami.' 'A jockey shouldn't drink,' said the rich man.

SEPTEMBER

7 Feet From A Spider

One day my office mate at Harvard Law School, Cara, mentioned to me that she'd read that we humans were never farther than seven feet away from a spider. At the time that seemed way too close for comfort. Now, having lived in the country for nine years, seven feet might as well be seven miles. My estimate based on personal experience is that one is never more than twelve inches away from a spider at any time.

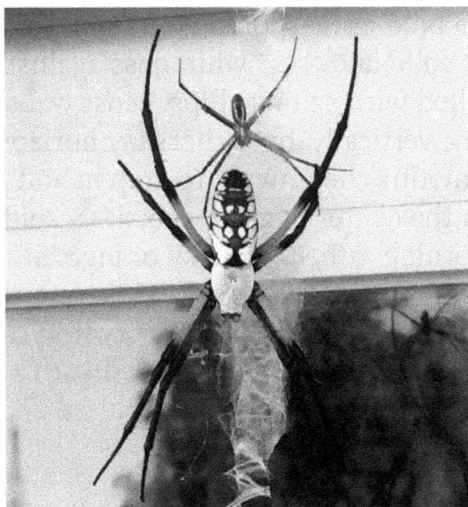

As a child I had such vivid nightmares starring spiders that I would wake up my sister with whom I shared a bedroom, for her help in searching the crumpled sheets for the giant, hairy and blood-thirsty creature I was sure was lurking above, below or *in* my bed, unblinking, waiting patiently as the Buddha for the lights to go out once again before pouncing.

As I got older the dreams faded and disappeared completely and I've made my peace with spiders. We share our house with the wolf, Brown Recluse, crab and a kind of spider we have affectionately nicknamed Bruisers because they are all neck and shoulders and ever ready to do battle. They really are quite cute.

I truly appreciate (most) spiders now and it's a good thing, too, because we might as well be running a spider farm so numerous are they in the fields and woods surrounding us.

On especially moist and humid mornings the webs in the fields stand out in stark relief, sparkling with delicate shiny beads. There are thousands of webs, stacked and packed in among the grasses like tenement houses. Some stand tall and proud and bold as flags on poles. From certain angles the webs look solid and their whiteness against the green is like a bay filled with sailing ships. Most webs hang in the traditional way, vertically, but others lay horizontally, tiny trampolines inviting the unwary to step in and jump around for a while. In the center of each web sits a spider. Some are pale as the morning, others a dusky orange. Still others are caustic yellow peppered with black. There are the disorganized webs looking like messy tufts of cotton candy. Other webs are meticulously spun as if created with a slide rule and a chalk reel. These are lovingly repaired and maintained by their house proud spiders.

Last summer my heart was stolen by a beautiful garden orb that made her home just under the eave of our garage. We watched her as if she were a documentary on PBS. In the mornings she'd work steadily and slowly to repair her web after the carnage from the previous night, after the violent death throe struggles of some unfortunate winged victim which was then sucked dry and unceremoniously dropped to the pavement below. By lunch her web was tidy and clean *nothing to see here!* and she sat at the center, looking sleepy and sated. But it was all an act. Ms. Orb was incredibly light and fast on her many feet.

Like supplicants Kel and I would bring her fresh horseflies.

The first time we did this she skittered to the top of her web and scrunched herself into a ball, hiding. But she soon learned that our approach meant a juicy meal and she would run towards our fingers as we placed the sacrifice into the sticky strands. She grew incredibly fat.

One day several suitors appeared (the male garden orbs are tiny in comparison to the females) and she had no interest in food. But then the males were gone - it would have been rude to ask where - and her appetite returned. Over time she produced an impressive five egg sacs, carefully securing each one to the side of the garage. She did such a tremendous job that the egg sacs stayed steady through the remainder of the summer, through the fall, the cold winds of winter and now into another summer.

Even though we knew the day was coming, Kel and I were heartbroken the morning the garden orb was gone. The web seemed achingly empty. It was still there, perfect. I checked throughout the day to see if perhaps she'd returned, but no, it had been her time and she went off to die alone and unseen. Eventually the pristine web fell into disrepair and disappeared completely. Only the eggs remained.

Sometime in the spring, the garden orb's five eggs "hatched." They are dented and empty now, looking like deflated beignets, but are still firmly secured to the garage. I would love to know where all of the little babies have gone, doing their good if grisly work out in the world. Wouldn't it be nice if one of her offspring took up residence in her mother's place? We could tell her stories about her strong and caring mama while tempting it with buzzing horseflies.

- September 1, 2016

Kinds of Flight

In the early evening as I watered the flower beds and the asparagus in the lingering heat, far off I could hear the wind come, leaves in distant trees hissing as it rushed towards me, growing in strength and volume, now swaying the trees nearby. It tugged at my hat and sent dried and crumpled leaves tumbling across the grass. The wind cleared away the oppressive heat and I looked upward expecting to see storm clouds. Instead, I saw a lone turkey vulture way up high, serene, floating, taking advantage of the new currents. Just below him, small black specks were wheeling and dipping under thin, gauzy clouds. Swallows, or some similar bird. I knew it from the way their wings curved back and from their quick darts and flashes of movement. There were probably 25 or 30 birds up there. For a while they stayed high above me in the same small area, simply enjoying the waves of wind. Young birds practicing their flying, perhaps, or joyfully shrugging off the dead stillness of the day and reveling in how the wind enhanced the freedom of flight.

In case you haven't realized by now, I love birds. We are lucky to get a good variety through here – some long-term residents, others that stay only a few days – and after a few years, my slow brain has caught on to the different types, when to expect them and their varied kinds of flight.

Our year-round residents, the chickadees, tufted titmouse and nuthatch flash nervously and quickly among the trees, always preferring the shelter of the branches to being exposed long in the open. The goldfinches come and go in flocks, one bird apparently guiding the movements of all. Egrets and herons lope across the skies in early morning and again in the early evening.

For aerial maneuvers it is hard to beat the Scissor-tailed Flycatchers (who are with us only during the summer months) or Bluebirds (year-round). Both are highly-skilled insect-hunters. They are the aerobatic pilots of our airspace, executing with precision steep banks and stomach-dropping free falls that follow the erratic zig-zag of insects in motion, snapping them up in mid-air. The Scissor-tails with their long tail feathers look like small kites fluttering against the blue. The sturdy Bluebirds are all business.

The heavier bodies of flickers and red-bellied woodpeckers are more difficult to keep aloft, or so it seems from their flying. They flap-flap-flap-flap, then glide for several beats, dropping precipitously before they hurriedly flap-flap-flap-flap again. I suspect they really prefer to be firmly attached to the side of a tree.

As for the crows, they are always in a hurry. Their flying is filled with purpose, flat, steady and powerful wing-beats carry them over fields and through the trees. Crows understand that the shortest distance between two points is a straight line. They prefer to be in their clans and often fly in pairs or small groups. Their flight seems to me tinged with guilt, skulking, and I am certain that they are either flying away or towards trouble.

The elusive stealth flyer of our skies is the Barn Owl. Just as the last tinges of light drain from the sky, the owl leaves his nest box up in the barn's rafters and glides silently out over the fields. The Barn Owl has fringed feathers with comb-like edges that break down turbulence and muffle sound. This silent flight is why he is so deadly to field mice, gophers and snakes. His coloring lets him fade into the night. They never see or hear him coming. Small mercies from the executioner.

Finally, perhaps my favorite flyer, the hawk. If the owl is the stealth plane the hawk certainly must be the fighter jet. He circles idly above, seemingly indifferent, just as the vultures do, but his fierce eyes are surveying the landscape far below, looking for the slightest ill-timed dash for freedom through the tall grass - and then down he swoops, claws and beak at the ready.

- September 2, 2011

Working the Seam

As a kid a glimpse from the car window of a horse-head pump nodding up and down in the middle of an open field sparked stories in my head that rolled along with the miles. It seemed to me then, as now, a starkly lonely sight. The pumps endured the battering of the elements, whether a functioning one, tirelessly, valiantly even, laboring on unnoticed or a defunct, still one, frozen where it stopped, abandoned to rust and the reaching weeds. Even the sound of the working pump, often the only thing to keep company with these machines, is lonely; an echoing clank of metal against metal, a sigh as the pipe slides down into the earth and back out.

Today three of these pumps share company with us on our ranch. There were four, but a couple of years ago a huge pit was dug and one was uprooted, its seeming miles of pipe pulled and pulled and pulled from deep in the ground and carted off to a graveyard of muddy and rusty oil field equipment. A Land of Misfit Parts. Aside from a deep, grassy impression, there is no evidence on our field now even of its existence. The other three pumps are mostly silent, but as far as we know, there is still oil below them to be reaped. We don't own the pumps and we don't own what's beneath them.

The view up close is less romantic than the my childhood

glimpses from the car window. Up close one sees the sludgy pools of oil, the rust that has stained the ground, workers' footprints set like fossils into the clay mud, busted gears, chunks of cracked and discarded metal, chips of plastic, oil-soaked rags and gloves. Gifts from the oilmen.

The power of these metal beasts is frightening with their gears and thick loops of belts, grumbling motors and hammering heads. The pumps, when in motion, are relentless. They won't stop for a man's arm or his skull. They pump on in the rain and under the bleach of the sun. They are alive that way, myopic, determined, alone. Working the seam.

- September 5, 2011

The Last Halloween

I remember the last time I went trick-or-treating. It was an unusually mild night for northeastern Ohio. No rain or hint of snow, just a light breeze and a softness to the air that I can still feel. It's a texture belonging solely to fall evenings before the leaves have left the branches. I can't remember if we had a flashlight, though we must have. It was dark out there along the dirt roads. No streetlamps or help from the lit windows of houses. They were set too far back behind the trees.

My best friend and I were allowed to go out by ourselves and to my enduring humiliation I wore the same costume worn the previous year and the same one worn by my sister the year before that: a stoplight made out of a big cardboard box. The box banged against my knees with every step and made walking slow. The cardboard rubbed uncomfortably against my arms and it was hot inside the box. Luckily for me my friend was similarly dressed in a box only hers was painted to look like a milk carton.

We crunched along the dirt road, talking about whatever tween girls talk about, swinging our trick-or-treat bags. Driveways were long and houses far apart, but the neighbors were typically generous and we reaped a decent amount of sugar that night. One very special neighbor handed me four of those huge, thick bars of Hershey's chocolate - one for me and one each for my siblings. (Yes, I did give them theirs, but the debate raged in my brain for a while. That amount of chocolate could've held me for a long time.)

From my adult perspective, that night has meaning, nurtured by the passing years and the changes of time, environment and tradition. A gentle wind rustling brittle leaves, the crunch of the gravel underfoot, our childish voices pressing into the dark, a lone, welcoming pumpkin set by a door, the flickering candle inside lending shadowy movement to its carved eyes and grinning mouth. A soft October night in Ohio. The last Halloween.

- September 7, 2011

Utah State Route 159

From about 11,000 feet, standing on the rock-strewn slopes of Wheeler Peak, the road we would take was too small to see, but other roads, threadlike, rolled out into the basin and disappeared. Green circles cut into the brown dryness, circles created by the sweep of giant sprinklers, turning like the hands of a clock. The wisps and strings of rain far off in the distance hung from thick gray clouds.

We came down from the mountain and east into tiny Baker and the improbable and welcome: espresso and veggie burgers. Four motorcycles were tethered like horses in front of what once could have been a saloon but now was a store and motel. We cruised briefly west before heading determinedly north, slipping out of Nevada and climbing back in a few hours later somewhere among the Goshute Mountains.

A faded sign pointed us towards Gandy, Trout Creek, Callao and the ghost town - or so it said on the map - of Gold Hill and shortly thereafter the pavement ended and we bumped onto gravel. Immediately a plume of mocha-colored dust flared out behind us. For a few slow seconds a crow kept pace with us and it seemed he might fly with us the whole way. Behind him bale fortresses of freshly-cut hay rose high in golden-brown squares. Evidence of a hard, grassless winter to come.

The road cut between mountain ranges, the valley wide and flat and to the right of us, ribbons of salt flats rippled and shimmered against the base of blue foothills. Trapped water. The Great Basin. The road is also wide and flat and every few miles thick groves of willows hide houses, barns, windmills and tractors. Patches of cattails and thick-bladed grasses gave clues to the hiding places of cold springs and the persistent trickle of water traveling down from high in the mountains. Vibrant life amid the dust and salt crust.

The landscape subtly changed as the road slowly rose and narrowed. We edged closer to the mountains towards the west. Hills flattened by distance unfolded into craggy canyons choked with blue-green pines and gray jutting slabs of rock. Thin trails spindled off in confused lines. Every sign we passed pointed to towns to the east as if there were nothing ahead, nothing to the west. Near Callao we stopped at an overgrown picnic area scraped out of the ground by the Civilian Conservation Corps. Wood tables slowly disappearing among the weeds and grass. A thin stream cut through the picnic area and then under the road, the water cold and clear. Gray feathers lay scattered along the banks and a lone beer can bobbed in the stony shallows.

Through another town: a faded house surrounded by junked cars and a rusting yellow bus splashed with the words, "Into the Wild" and then briefly back onto pavement that began and ended at a neat Mormon ward house.

We turned in earnest then towards the mountains, climbing, a sign pointing now towards the west and Ibapah. Other signs appeared and through binoculars we could make out a gate and an airstrip. Maybe. The map told us only: *The Utah Test and Training Range*.

At last we reached Gold Hill and its broken down buildings, scarred hills and remnants of the mining town it once was. Not quite a ghost town. A man in a white t-shirt stacked wood in his backyard and stopped to watch, hands on hips, as we drove past.

A turned over garbage can - a long way from home - identified itself in white spray paint as "Ibapah," its contents spilling out along the roadside. For some reason we stopped and got out to look at it then righted it and wheeled it to the edge of the road. The can marked our turn and the end of the dirt road. 93A. We turned right onto smooth pavement and bit by bit what we call civilization rose up against the mountains marking the horizon: a billboard, phone service and radio stations, an on ramp, rushing cars, Wendover.

As ever, when writing, I am indebted to Cactus Ed. When I look west, I do so through his eyes.

...to make the discovery of the self in its proud sufficiency which is not isolation but an irreplaceable part of the mystery of the whole. Come on in. The earth, like the sun, like the air, belongs to everyone - and to no one.

- Edward Abbey, from *The Journey Home*

- September 17, 2011

A Short Work of Fiction (Tilt-A-Whirl)

It wouldn't be long before they got here. In a small town a death is reason for hurry; homicide assures great speed. And they would all come, the off-duty and the ones who could only dream they were cops. Certainly the radios were humming now. *That city woman killed someone.* The man had meant to do me harm, of that I have no doubt, but would they believe me? My ties here are thin. I've kept to the outskirts. I came from elsewhere.

As I sit waiting for them I know I should be planning for the critical moments to come. A resolute silence, a lawyer and then a calm and clear statement of what had happened, but my mind keeps pulling my thoughts back to the summer after college when a friend and I went together to a carnival near my hometown. It was raining lightly but not enough to have brought the rides to a halt and we gave the tall and too-thin, bearded man our tickets to ride the Tilt-A-Whirl.

The yellow clowns painted on the sides of the cars were vaguely sinister yet alluring, the deep red metal of the clam-shaped cars shiny with rain. As the ride began we moved ourselves from side to side, urging the car to spin. Before long the ride was in full motion and we pressed together and clutched at the wheel in the center. When it would spin crazily tears of laughter poured down our faces. We laughed so hard there was no sound to it. Our grins flashing by must have looked maniacal to the spectators standing around the outside of the ride. To us the people were merely colorful blurs.

The tall carny, seeing our efforts, worked his way towards us on the slick and undulating surface until he was standing in front of our car. He grabbed the side and shoved it, sending us into a blissful spiral, but then suddenly he was gone, his footing lost in the rain. He had slipped over the edge of the ride. For a few moments more the ride continued, mechanically oblivious to what had happened. My friend and I strained to see him, hoped to see him standing, unharmed. Later we'd learned he'd broken an arm and was bruised and cut. The joy in the day was gone, our thoughts playing over and over the image of the man disappearing over the side of the ride. We felt we'd done it to him with our stupid quest for the sensation of spinning.

The afternoon light is soft and gray coming into the window. The house is so quiet. Soon it will be filled with strangers and the sounds that strangers make. I rest my hands on the table and study the fingers. They're thin and white. They're thin and white and mine and they pulled the trigger.

- September 20, 2011

Evening Walks

It's dark by 8 pm now. There is the thinnest filament of cool threaded through the warm summer wind, which now comes more frequently from the northeast than from the south. A fall wind. Cool air collects in shallow hollows. Yellow and brown dot the trees and the rattling sound of curled sycamore leaves clinging to their branches contains the germ of future ice storms and bitter, sweeping winds. The night jars still wheel and dip in the twilight, but they'll be gone by October, replaced by Canada geese on the wing, heading south.

No matter. The evening walks will go on. A ritual created by the presence of Ike and his requirements for exercise, for exploring, for chasing and playing. Turns out we require those things, too. He is endlessly fascinated by the cows who briefly hold their ground, then amble off at the last moment, looking back at him reproachfully. And the rabbit that lives in the woods near the oil pump and the armadillo who, despite Ike's thundering run, makes good his escape every time.

Last night there were many things to see: a skunk nosing the grass and dirt in the upper pasture; a very irritated Western Pygmy Rattler soaking up the last of the day's heat; ten or twelve poor-wills circling over the pasture; a new pile of bones under a cedar tree and Ike discovered the fun of jumping into the new pond and out again while his friend, Winston, stood stoically and dry on the shore. Winston, the neighbor's dog, sometimes joins us for both our morning and evening walks and is teaching Ike the grave seriousness of patrolling one's territory.

It's not quite yet, but it soon will be, the most lovely, the most melancholy time of the year. As summer loosens its blazing grip, as the days shorten and evenings cool into purple, the sense of time passing - of the past - heightens. It's a delicate season. Its bittersweet flavor makes it my favorite, yet I also dread its coming. And still...is there a place of perpetual fall? If so, I might like to live there and walk each evening through the twilight.

- September 21, 2011

Dizzy Dean Days

On a beautiful October day a few years back we arrived at our new home in rural Oklahoma and while we waited for the moving van to appear, we noticed that our secluded road seemed awfully busy. That weekend we kept seeing shiny vintage cars and restored tractors heading towards what seemed to us as the middle of nowhere. A few days later we saw the same line of cars and tractors heading back in the other direction. The middle of nowhere turned out to be Spaulding, and Spaulding, we found out, was once home to Jay Hanna "Dizzy" Dean.

Dizzy Dean? With no internet connection set up and the word "smartphone" not yet part of the cultural lexicon, I did what I usually do when I need the answer to an urgent question. I called my dad. As usual, he had an answer: Dizzy Dean was a major league pitcher for the Cardinals and the Cubs. Became a sportscaster. As a kid, dad plied* the stands at the old Cleveland Stadium and now, despite looking as if he's napping during televised sporting events, he's got a near encyclopedic grasp of football, basketball and baseball. He could probably tell me a thing or two about old cars and tractors as well, if only I asked.

Born in Arkansas in 1910, Jay and his family moved to Spaulding in 1925 and even though Jay wasn't enrolled in the local school, he and his brother Paul, played for the junior high team. He further honed his pitching by hurling hickory nuts at squirrels. Anyway, every year the good folks of Spaulding have a 2-day event that celebrates Dean, and maybe long ago it really was about honoring him.

As the son of a sharecropper who picked cotton alongside his father and siblings, Dean would've fit in comfortably with the current residents of Spaulding. But as Dean retreats further into the sepia past, the days reserved in his honor now celebrate rural life: farming and ranching and independence and catching up with one's neighbors – and the accouterments of such. John Deere tractors, bailers, dusky mules, muscled steers and fried pickles. Throw in a few lovingly restored, scrubbed and buffed vintage Chevys and Fords – all fins and pointy taillights – and there you have Dizzy Dean Days.

*Dad elaborates:
I worked as an usher, but didn't seat people. In those days, there was a rope dividing general admission seats from reserved seats. For the first four innings I watched to see that no one climbed over the generals to the reserved [seats]. If they did (unless they were my buddies), I called a nearby cop. It was a great job! I worked from 1947 through 1949. The Indians were in the American League, Dean was in the National League. I did see him, but not as a player. I did see many of the great ones.

- September 22, 2011

Learn more about Dizzy Dean at dizzydean.com. Or, ask your own dad. Incidentally, did athletes trash talk in the '30s and '40s? Yes. Yes, they did and Dizzy's got some great quotes.

A Perfect Circle: Goodbye to R.E.M.

It's fitting that the person who introduced me to R.E.M. is the same one who told me that after 31 years together, they'd called it quits. I remember very distinctly that I was reluctant to go see them when they came through Cleveland in 1984 (July 10, to be precise; *Dream Syndicate* opened). I don't remember why I was reluctant, but my friend convinced me to go. They performed at The Variety Theater, a small venue on Lorain Avenue that had seen better days. There were a lot of empty seats at the back of the theater and the bands' friends and girlfriends sold t-shirts near the lobby. Michael Stipe hadn't yet perfected his stage persona and he merely stood behind the microphone, clutching the stand, looking as if he was trying hard to pretend the audience wasn't out there. He wore a white button-down shirt and his face and long curly hair were softened and blued by the stage lights. The combination of his obscure (and hard to understand) lyrics and rich voice with a touch of the south pulled us into a small, intimate circle. He was mesmerizing. By the time the show ended, I was hooked. Like patients slowly coming out of ether, my friends and I sat in the car afterwards listening to *Murmur*, reluctant to shake the spell.

I listened to them practically non-stop from that point on. I collected interviews and articles, clipped photos, wasted hours in front of MTV hoping to see their videos and even developed a small cottage industry around my obsession - creating pen and ink portraits of Stipe (with a loyal customer base of two). If I sound like a 1960s teenager in the throes of Beatlemania, that wouldn't be too far off. (Understandable at my age, but the older and ostensibly more rational felt the same way. A music critic wrote in a review of *Murmur* that angels in heaven wouldn't be strumming harps, they'd be playing R.E.M. songs on Rickenbacker guitars.).

R.E.M. was the dominant band on my personal Generation X soundtrack. Through them I learned about Patti Smith, Athens, Georgia and the folk artist, Reverend Howard Finster. I saw R.E.M. another six times and (through the same intrepid friend) met them backstage at another Cleveland concert (1985; *The Three O'Clock* opened). I still have the album cover with their signatures.

I carried my love for R.E.M. to college with me. The EP *Chronic Town* is inextricably linked with my freshman year, windows opened wide at night to let in the late summer air and an overworked small radio/tape player splattered with oil paint (I was an art major.). I sought out local bands that covered their songs. I found another benefactor to buy my R.E.M.-related artwork and hitched a ride with a guy named Blaze to see them at the Taft Theater in Cincinnati in 1986 (*Fetchin' Bones* opened). As thanks I gave him the trampled $20 bill I found on the floor after the show.

The blush began to retreat slightly from the rose during my senior year when R.E.M. came to my university. It's not that I wasn't thrilled they would perform there, I was just saddened that they'd gone mainstream. They had to have if they were including my pink-and-mint-green, preppy university on their tour schedule. I didn't even join my friends sleeping in line the night before tickets went on sale (but I did get a ticket nevertheless...). And when a fellow classmate appeared on stage next to Stipe, signing to *King of Birds*, I was thoroughly hurt and offended. You bet your sweet bippy I was jealous! It should've been me up there except for the fact that I didn't know sign language and as a shy and inept teenager, I wouldn't have had a clue as to how to get myself up on stage anyway.

As the years passed, R.E.M. inevitably toyed with their signature sound just enough to alienate me, committing the ultimate unpardonable betrayal of favorite band to loyal fan who was "with them from the beginning."

Just as fatal, I wasn't interested in knowing their politics or hearing which celebrities they were mingling with at parties. I guess I got stuck back in 1984: the indecipherable lyrics, the shy, curly-haired singer with the gentle voice, the sweet hope of friends selling band t-shirts on a fold-up table and the sound of *Perfect Circle* playing through the speakers of a darkened car on a July night in the parking lot of The Variety Theater.

Goodbye R.E.M...and thanks to L for bringing me to them.

- September 23, 2011

A Trip Into Town

Our first stop is always the post office because we're never really sure what time it closes. 4:30? 5:00? The long-haired clerk and I play a little game together every time I mail a package. After putting the package on the scale, he says: *I can guarantee this for Monday for only $52.85* (I look aghast) *or I can possibly get it there by Monday, but most likely Tuesday for $22.45* (I mumble that there's really no hurry), *or I can get it there by Wednesday for $4.23* (I nod enthusiastically, yet feel like a cheapass). He knows I will never pay the highest price and I know that he's got to go through the litany of absurd choices (plus the singsong: "anything liquid, fragile or perishable?"), especially when his manager is standing a few feet away. But he has a slight smile on his lips as he rattles off the numbers.

At the feed store we got a collar for Ike. His linebacker neck just keeps getting bigger. And a bright orange leash to keep in the car in case we ever forget to bring one with us (which I had). I also wanted a big bag of black oil sunflower seeds for the birds, but the storeowner said they were too expensive to stock (*"They went up to $35 a bag and no one was buying them."*), but he said he'd have smaller bags later in the fall. Meanwhile folks were feeding their birds other kinds of seeds, he said. Kel picked up turnip seeds for the garden and we almost got out of there with only those items, except then Kel went out to see if the new collar would fit Ike and that gave me just enough time to find the shoe and boot section of the store. *Interesting*, I thought. Kel came back in and I joined him at the counter, my mind working. When Kel opened his wallet to pay, the owner asked, fatefully, *"Is that it?"* and I blurted out that I would've picked up a pair of Bogs boots if only they'd had my size. He reared back a bit and assumed an expression of deep hurt. Pushing himself away from the counter he cried, *"Your size! What's your size? Of course we have your size!"* and down the aisle we went, past the rat poison, the packs of spider traps, the horse halters and the numbered ear tags (for cows) and he leaned down and looked at each and every dusty box of Bogs until he found one that said: Kids 5, Black. He handed me the box and pointed to a cracked black chair in the corner near a tall pile of cardboard boxes. Then he grabbed a plastic grocery bag to put on my foot since I wasn't wearing socks. He fretted over me so much I flashed back briefly to Nordstrom's shoe department: ensconced in a deeply-cushioned lounge chair while listening to classical music being played on the piano near the escalators. Someone was just about to come around with a tray of champagne when I "came to" and found I was still at a feed store in Oklahoma that smelled strongly of fertilizer, in a shell of a town, sitting on a broken chair wearing a grocery bag on my foot printed with the words, *ThankYouThankYouThankYou*. I got the boots.

Later, in line at Walmart (where they had bags of black oil sunflower seeds, same price as always), the cashier was telling the wrinkled couple in front of me how much she hated snakes and the old man was teasing her by inviting her to come out and sit by the pond and watch the snakes sunning themselves on the rocks. She kept saying, *"No, no! I'm not comin' to visit you!"* The old man just laughed with his tongue pointing straight out of his mouth while his wife, the buying transaction over, gently urged him and their cart towards the exit. When I approached the counter I told the cashier she wouldn't want to come visit me since we had lots of snakes, too. When she asked and I told her where we lived, she said, *"I can't go anywhere! They're snakes north, south, east and west of me! I just hate snakes! Doesn't matter if they're only on TV, I hate them!"* I pushed the cart out into the sun and the hot parking lot, thinking about snakes, and Kel loaded the bag of sunflower seeds.

While Kel got the squishy right front tire on the car looked at, I took Ike (on his new orange leash) for a walk along the old railroad tracks and the small garden someone planted there. There were rows of okra in bloom and tall tomato plants that looked healthy but had not a single flower nor ripening fruit. Then Ike and I found a shady alley to walk along and were greeted by the heavy, sweet fragrance of honeysuckle. The vine had overwhelmed a crape myrtle. I prefer the honeysuckle anyway.

Kel pulled up in the car, tire repaired, and we decided to take the dirt road back home since the car wasn't clean anyway. We'd seen a plume of dark gray smoke rising from the south and though it looked close when we'd first seen it, it seemed to recede farther and farther to the south as we drove towards it.

- September 27, 2011

OCTOBER

Sundance, The Point of the Mountain and A Day Away

August skies are lullabies/promises to keep
dandelions and twisting vines/clover at your feet
memories of aspen leaves/trembling in the wind
honeybees and fantasies/where to start again
some place cool an' green an' shady

– John Denver, *Cool an' Green an' Shady*

It happened on an otherwise normal Thursday at around 5:30 pm just as we were about to sit down to dinner and midway through a phone conversation the kind of which I'd had one too many of in the previous weeks. What had been on a slow simmer began to boil. My last nerve was shot. I was suffering from road rage, sidewalk rage, apartment-building-hallway rage – not to mention grocery aisle rage – and for the next few hours I fumed and moped around our apartment, feeling deeply sorry for myself. Ike crawled under his side table "cave" and Kel nodded solemnly at my every curse and intoned, "Yes, dear. Yes, dear," a hopeful mantra designed to stave off the meltdown he could see coming. The long evening walk didn't help. A cup of hot chocolate was hopeful, but made barely a break in the dense clouds of my foul mood.

Then a few hours after the phone call it hit me: I was seriously stressed out. I needed a change of scenery and fast. Luckily, a remedy was already in the works. It was time to go where the air is thin and clean, the sky a piercing blue and where the wind holds an icy touch of the winter to come: *the mountains.* By 10 am the next morning we were headed up to Bobby Redford's little retreat in the Wasatch, Sundance.

The winding road up to the resort is a therapy of its own. One must concentrate on where the car is, there's no space for anger or stress. Sundance is tucked into the hills and amongst tall trees and despite the fact that there are restaurants, a screening room, art studios, cabins and homes (not to mention ski lifts and runs), it feels very secluded and small and homey. Fall, in my opinion, is the perfect time to go. Interspersed among the yellow-leaved aspens that blanket the mountainsides are bright dots of red, orange and deep green. We wandered around the resort and then treated ourselves to "wet" (no foam) soy lattes and settled onto a bench outside to watch the Beautiful People go by. Because the tram up to the top of the mountain (and to hiking trails) doesn't allow dogs, we finished up our lattes and decided to do our hiking elsewhere.

The road beyond Sundance is switchbacked and extremely narrow. It felt as if our car was skimming the edge of the road as vehicles coming the other direction drove past us. I missed a lot of the scenery while hugging the road, but Kel reports that it was spectacular. When we reached the Timpanogos trailhead and the hiking route up to Stewart Falls we stopped for a picnic lunch at the old amphitheater hidden among the pines, then we pulled on our day packs and headed up. The total 4-mile hike up and back to Stewart Falls took us about two hours.

On the way home we decided to take a short detour to visit The Point of the Mountains. Kel had been reading a lot about paragliding lately and we learned that one of the premier spots in the country for the sport is right here in Utah. When we arrived, it wasn't looking good. There were only a couple of cars in the parking lot and two guys gazing forlornly out from the high plateau down to the valley spread out below. Two gliders lay still strapped to the tops of the cars, wrapped up tight like canvas burritos. There wasn't a breath of wind.

While Kel went off to interrogate Man Number One, Man Number Two suddenly appeared beside me and Ike. We started talking about dogs and soon enough Dave, a hang-glider and instructor of 41 years, offered to take me up on his glider once the wind was right. My mother didn't raise a fool and I simply laughed it off and let Ike pull me away from the salesman pressure for a bit. Before long, Kel and Dave and I and Man Number One were talking wind and gliders and geography and how silly and foolish paragliders were as compared to hang-gliders.

Man Number One decided to set up his glider just in case the wind changed and Dave got to talking about thermals and how thermals were all about contrasts: dirt and pavement; high ground and low; heat and cool; light and dark. I got it, but my mind wandered anyway. The view out there was just too big, too beautiful. Endless sky above, a long, flat valley below with the mighty artery of I-15 splitting it in two, pulsing and teeming with rush hour cars headed for home, north and south. To the east the Wasatch buckled and climbed. To the west lay the hazy shimmer of the Great Salt Lake. As Dave's voice morphed into a pleasant hum of white noise, my eyes drifted upwards and I saw a large hawk circling high above the field on which we stood. He was gliding effortlessly, wheeling in the air without moving a single feather. No doubt it looked down upon us poor humans with pity and mirth. Our puny wingspans, our heavy burden called gravity. There was no doubt in my mind that his presence above the well-known hang-gliding and paragliding site was no accident. He was shoving his winged freedom in our faces.

At some point, Dave set up his glider and offered to let me slip into the upside down hammock-suit "just to get a feel" for things. Once I felt how comfortable it was he was pretty sure I'd be asking to take the glider for a spin with him. (For the low, low price of $100.) I hung out in the hammock-suit for a while, feeling stupid, and then all at once a strong breeze rose over the plateau. I looked across the field and saw paragliders everywhere, their colorful parachutes billowing and collapsing, rising and falling. Some fliers were already strapped into their funny "seats" that resemble turtle shells, some dragging their chutes to the edge of the field where they would step off and hope to be lifted into the air. Already gliders were circling above us, seeking the hawk's thermal. They made their slow way along the edge of the plateau and up and up, heading east and then west again, then east. Some of them were high above, looking as if they were going to touch their toes along the mountain's edge. We feared the gliders – so close together – would collide and fall, but somehow they all missed each other. I extricated myself from the hammock and soon enough we saw Dave climb into his suit and lope off carrying his hang-glider. He walked slowly and with effort along the thin gravel runway at the end of which is a sign imbedded into the ground that admonishes pilots to "Hook In." Dave stood at the edge for a minute and then he was off the ground, soaring, moving with a speed and purpose unmatched by the paragliders.

He looked like a giant bird. For a tiny second I wished I had hooked in next to him, but the solid earth felt pretty good under my feet. He seemed to be heading straight for the sun. I watched him for a while and then looked back above the field and then above the mountains, but the hawk was gone. There were only humans flying.

- October 3, 2013

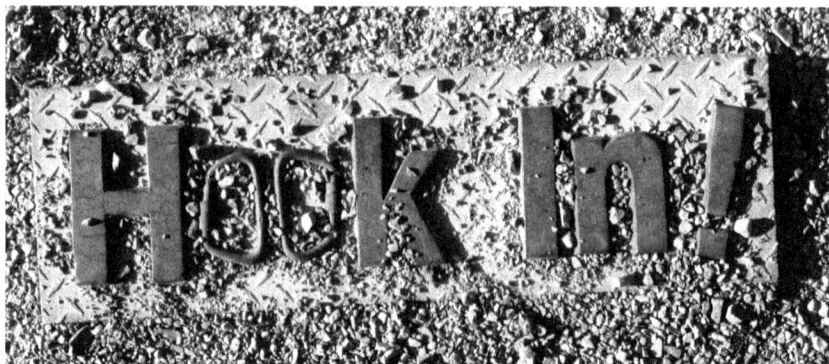

122

Memories Of A Passenger

These days I'm either behind the wheel or riding shotgun, but as a kid I spent a lot of hours as a passenger in the back seat of the family car. Many of those years were spent wedged into the middle, being both the youngest and smallest, able to see only the ribbon of road ahead. But sometimes I got to sit next to a window and as the excitement of the road trip ebbed and we all became lulled to silence by the engine and the miles, I'd look out the window, gathering impressions like a dog taking in the scents flowing into an open window, tantalizing his nose.

There were the white farm houses, neat as pins, mere feet from the road with barns and outbuildings jumbled behind; tractors, shining silos, crooked fence posts and every once in a while a horse hanging its head over the side to get at the sweet, long grass. There were acres and acres of corn, tall and green. Farm stands and historical markers which we noted but never stopped to read, rest areas with rough and faded picnic tables and toilets that were nothing but dark and frightening holes in the ground.

Those were the days of Stuckey's – the purveyor of pecan logs – whose green roof beckoned one in for a bathroom break and something sweet. When Holiday Inn was *the* hotel and elusive at that, with its sign a beacon in the night, bristling with light bulbs and topped with a star. A night in a hotel assured that my brother and I would push the ice machine button repeatedly and stand mesmerized in front of the candy machine, the treats so close yet so far. A cruel taunt to the coinless.

There was the town with the red caboose parked in the square. The many anonymous playgrounds where we'd swing or teeter-totter and never see again. Bologna sandwiches eaten along the side of a quiet road, batting at mosquitoes. Wet footprints on the cement around sparkling blue, kidney-shaped hotel pools. Lying in bed at night, feeling even then the loneliness of the sound of trucks passing on the highway.

I still love road trips, but some of that road magic is gone. Maybe it's because now I have to pay attention to signs, other cars and the gas gauge, or maybe it's the difference between sitting in the front of the car, or being squeezed into the back, nestled against my brothers and sister.

- October 7, 2011

U.S. Route 50

A missed exit at Wichita sent us seventy-seven miles towards the northeast when we should've been heading southwest. It meant two additional hours behind the wheel. There was some steering-wheel-pounding and a little bit of creative verbalization, but without the error we wouldn't have picked up where we left off years ago, continued to connect dots on the map. We wouldn't have seen some of the heart of Kansas.

Back in 2007 we'd taken 50 all the way from Washington, DC to Route 177 and into the Tall Grass Prairie, then south down 177 to I-35 on to Oklahoma and our new home. We were driving the heavily loaded, growling and comfort-challenged Ford F350 diesel. Highway 50 is a smooth two-laner that comes up against stop lights, slows you down to 35 MPH through the towns, and frustrates occasionally with local drivers in battered pick-ups who you know are thinking (as you ride their back bumper), "What's the all-fire hurry??" You have to lift your foot off of the gas pedal and adopt the same attitude. There really is no hurry.

This time of year the wide, flat fields of Kansas offer acres of corn – or the stubble of harvested corn, cows grazing among the dried and bent stalks – sorghum, cotton, something green and viney that might be soybeans and of course, sunflowers. It's peak sunflower season right now and the Kansas roads are brightened on both sides by swaying, sunny yellow. They're the wild, self-seeding kind and thick as weeds.

As on any road trip, the houses, stores, signs and people dispersed along this portion of 50 were fleeting and colorful blurred images, some committed to permanent time-place snapshots in the mind, others eventually getting jumbled into other times, other trips. There was the sign along the road that said: *"Feeding the World."* The tall and sturdy pale stone church flanked by two stone outhouses. I imagined black widow spiders lurking patiently under the seats. Another sign announced: *"Westward-Ho Round-Up Suppers!"* and at Walton we stopped for gas and walked the dog down a brick sidewalk. At the end of a long dirt driveway, a boy in a baseball cap played with his dog and further on, three people had gotten out of their car to pet a calf through a fence. *Tourists.*

There was the town with acres of quails and pheasants in huge covered coops. The birds looked like tawny showgirls strutting inside miniature, translucent circus tents. I lost count of the stinking, dusty feedlots, cows standing on piles of manure, cows lined up at troughs, cows lying in the hot sun of midday without a lick of shade in sight.

There were endless hay bales, in both bright greens and dull browns. High stacks of loose hay like loaves of rustic bread and hay rounds looking as if they are about to roll themselves across the flat fields.

The dirt roads that rumble off of 50 are named simply: Road A, Road J, Road F, etc. But not in alphabetical order. There's a puzzle and allure to dirt roads that makes me want to follow each one, except for my tendency to want to keep driving once in the car, to keep moving.

At Holcomb, I felt a nagging recognition. The name rang a distant bell and I thought at first it was because there is a giant Tyson's meatpacking plant there, but when I did a quick Internet search the name Clutter came up and I remembered that Truman Capote had written *In Cold Blood* about the Clutter family, brutally murdered in 1959 for a hidden fortune in a safe that never was.

Nearing our stopping point for the night, the smoke of a

wild fire outside of Dodge City marred the perfect blue of the sky and the next day's paper told the story. We were welcomed into Dodge City by a metal sculpture, high on a hill, of cowboys on horseback, swinging lassos. Signs encouraged us to visit the Boot Hill Museum. The main road into town is named Wyatt Earp and is lined with motels, Mexican restaurants, tattoo parlors and auto repair shops.

In the morning, we were back in the car and back on 50 heading west towards Garden City. I don't remember much of 50 from there. My mind and the map had moved on to Colorado, onto crossing those deceptive brown plains and climbing high into the mountains, away from the bobbing flatland sunflowers and into red rock country, up and up and eventually into glowing clusters of yellow aspens and carpets of dark green pine.

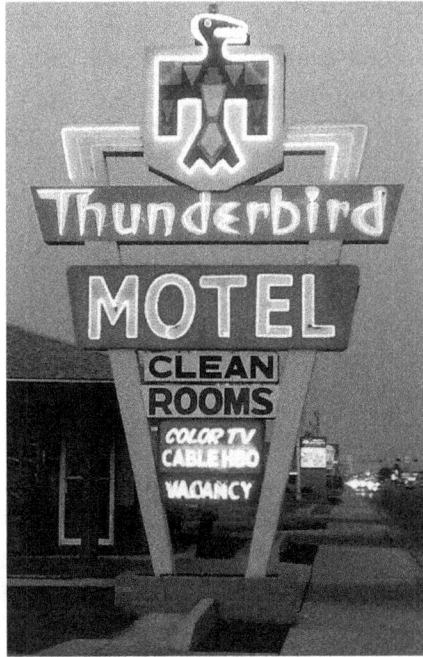

- October 8, 2011

This piece first appeared on Technorati.

We've traveled 50 through Kansas a few times since this trip, including venturing into Holcomb and up to the long driveway up to the Clutter's home where a No Trespassing sign stopped us from getting closer.

Waiting for Rain

Looking back over my blog and at my garden journal (my last entry was July 9, the day Ike came into our lives), I realize that I haven't had much to say about dirt lately. That might be because every plant in my perennial beds looks as if spent a minute too long under the broiler. Trees have prematurely lost their leaves. The cracks and splits in the pastures and gardens resemble miniature San Andreas Faults. Even the grasshoppers are having a tough time finding something green and succulent on which to feast. The brutal summer of 2011 has turned into a stingy, dry fall.

That's why we got so excited two days ago. We'd been watching the forecast for days, anticipating a fairly strong chance at some rain over the weekend. Saturday afternoon the radar showed a gloriously huge system bloated with dark greens and ominous pinks coming our way. It stretched from Minnesota down into Texas. It couldn't possibly miss us! That morning I had planned to thoroughly water the flower beds, but decided to let Mother Nature do the heavy lifting. She does a much better job of really getting the water where it needs to go anyway. We made sure the rain gauge was up, took the lid off of the rain collection barrel, stowed the lawnmower and anything else that might get damaged in the deluge. By early evening brooding gray clouds hung low in the sky and the wind had picked up. Midway through our post-dinner walk with Ike an even stronger breeze brought cool temperatures sweeping through and the air became heavy and smelled deliciously of moisture. We lingered outside, hoping to feel those first cold drops on our bare arms. We wouldn't have minded at all getting soaking wet.

We went to bed fully expecting to be woken by the staccato of rain on the roof and booming thunder. At one point in the night I was sure I heard rain, but when we woke in the morning, it was as quiet as every morning has been for months. And though the grass was slightly wet – we did get a smattering of rain overnight – the rain gauge was stubbornly empty. Checking the radar once again we saw that the giant system, so promising, had given up its west-to-east course and drifted south, showering Texas. Texas badly needed it. I don't begrudge them a single drop, but how I miss the sound and feel of rain!

Having grown up in the rain-and-snow-belt of northeastern Ohio, having had many a summer ruined by cold temperatures and gloomy skies, I've taken precipitation for granted – resented it more often than not as an annoyance and an inconvenience. Until we moved here, I've never looked forward to having rain come, to hoping that a forecast for a measly 20% chance would somehow materialize into an all-day soaker to nourish and revive all the creatures that so depend on water, including us, even though we don't have leaves and roots. I miss the feeling of warmth and safety one feels while watching a storm from the cozy interior of the house. Sunny days are treasures, no doubt about it and blue skies are the blank canvas for daydreaming and thoughts of flight and freedom, but rain... Rain is a balm. Rain is what makes us appreciate the sun and empty blue skies.

The pen really is mighty. Last night we had a steady, gentle rain that lasted for hours. The air is cool and clean. And the rain gauge this morning shows 1 ½".

- October 10, 2011

The Hackberry Tree

Cows shelter under it during the heat of the day and rub their huge heads against it. No doubt other animals have taken refuge under its spreading branches and gnarled roots. It presides over a shallow puddle of a pond, dry and cracked now. A tenacious, thorny vine with speckled leaves clings to it, reaching up into its sturdy branches. Single-strand barbed wire, coated with flaking rust was twisted around the tree some time ago and is slowly being absorbed into it. Nails have been pounded into it, remnants of bustling activity, tantalizing clues, other traces of which are long gone. It may be 20 years old or 50. Oklahoma trees take a beating – ice storms, drying southerly winds, harsh sun. It's difficult to tell the age of them.

One evening in late summer, Ike and I sat under the hackberry tree. Ike wasn't playfully biting at my sleeve or running ahead and I felt no particular urge to be anywhere else. For a few minutes we had our own kind of roots and were still. We surveyed the dry little pond and the humps and hillocks, the fading sky and the black flash of crows brushing the horizon. For a few minutes, we saw what the hackberry sees.

- October 13, 2011

A Greenhouse for Winter

Neither one of us can remember if we bought the greenhouse in 2008 or 2009. Either way, it's been a project that's hung over our heads for too long. Kel found the ad on *craigslist* and we drove into Oklahoma City to take a look at it. The man selling it – we called him Patio Joe because he was in the pond business (think koi and lily pads) – took us to his back yard and there it was, an oxidizing metal skeleton with its various parts strewn around, some in buckets, some heaped in piles. Joe lost the greenhouse mojo somewhere along the way and had never finished putting it up. (We would later relate very well to losing one's greenhouse mojo.) Black plastic shelving lined the open walls. Kel examined it carefully and then we drove away, getting only a few miles before deciding to make an offer. Joe accepted and we told him we'd be back the next day to disassemble it.

It took us two days in the hot sun to do it and Kel said that we should be taking pictures and we should be marking the parts so that we could more easily put it all back together, but we didn't mark anything and we took only a handful of photos. (None of which, by the way, actually helped at all later. As the official photographer, I can say this.) The second day I was sunburned and my muscles were sore, but the hard part was over. We loaded everything onto a flatbed trailer that we'd borrowed from a guy we knew who ran cattle and headed home.

Everything was unloaded into the barn and there it all sat, a victim of inertia and to unforeseen bumps in the road that kept us from immediately putting it all back together again. Then last spring we finally got after it and fairly quickly we had holes in the ground and the pipes cemented into place. Beams and crossbeams were bolted together. It started looking like a greenhouse. We put down sheets of black plastic to kill the grass inside and then fall came with its high winds and circumstances took us away from Oklahoma for a long while.

This fall the mornings have been calm so we've been able to work on unfurling the long, thick rolls of plastic that will cover the structure. I didn't think that the two of us alone could do it without sailing away or getting tangled in the sheeting. Kel as usual does the really hard and heavy parts and I watch nervously, ready to dial 911. So far three sides of plastic are up and flapping a bit in the late afternoon breeze. I have no idea how we are going to get the top covered.

But now I'm getting excited, finally seeing it come together. We already have things to move into it: fig trees, lemon, lime and grapefruit plants, a big pot of lemongrass that I have for cooking but can't bring myself to cut and use and pots of rosemary and various kinds of thyme. I'm looking forward to having fresh greens available throughout most of the year, to getting a jump on spring planting, to having tomatoes tied to the rafters next summer, heavy with fruit, and to carrots and radishes safe from nibbling varmints and whatever else we can coax to grow there.

Side four should go up today - wind and bodies willing - then we'll tackle the top. We can see the light at the end of the greenhouse. Just in time, too. Winter is coming.

- October 17, 2011

A Tomb is Opened in Oklahoma

It must have been a little like Howard Carter breaking into King Tut's tomb, albeit on the scale of, say, a flea relative to a blue whale, but nevertheless an exciting moment: when the first shafts of light and the fresh 2011 breeze met the stale 1990-or-so air and mingled, sending dust wheeling and moving for the first time in 20 odd years, revealing untold treasures, a dark and musty mystery coming to light.

The place had sat just as it had been left for an unknown number of years, who knows why. Perhaps the original owner just got tired and one day he turned the lock on the door and never came back. A *For Sale* sign was taped to the glass, yellowing in the corner of one window. Year after year layers of dirt and grime obscured what was inside, but one could still see well enough to discern the stocked shelves and the aisles leading off towards the back of the store, the large sales counter off to one side.

And then one day, an enterprising citizen bought the store, lock, stock and barrel. All of the nails, screws, paints, elbow joints and hammers. The wire, electrical switches, door knobs, screwdrivers and *No Trespassing* signs. Even old calendars and "point of purchase" bumper stickers that had sat on the sales counter for tens of years. If not the opulent items of gold and jewels, the pots of honey and spices and figurines of servants required by the pharoah's spirit to carry with him into the afterworld, they are at least useful items for everyday life here on planet earth.

Kel and I went in the other day. We *had* to. Not because we needed anything (there are two existing, competing stores in town anyway), but because we had to see for ourselves the treasures that had been locked up inside the tomb for all of those years. Was the new owner really going to try and sell that old stuff (yes)? Were the prices going to be rock-bottom to move them off of the shelves (no)? Was he going to clean off the dust (no)? Would the new owner and his family be cursed for generations because they had violated this sacred hardware resting place (have to wait and see on that one)?

Indeed there were piles of dated goodies, and in the back, beyond the reach of mere mortal customers was a dark chamber filled to the top with cardboard boxes. More riches. A tall shelf in the back was crisscrossed with (mummy's cloth?!) strips of gauzy, white fabric and was embellished with handwritten signs on lined paper ripped from a notebook admonishing: *Not for sale today* and *Copper Not for Sale this Week.*

We didn't buy anything and the owner didn't seem troubled by it. In fact he hardly noticed us at all. His was the attitude of distraction one would expect from an archeologist tending his precious discovery. As we left a man came in, another tourist seeking the thrills of the newly opened vault into the past. He stopped just inside the door, scanned the length and breadth of the place, took off his ball cap and slowly rubbed his head in wonder.

- October 21, 2011

NOVEMBER

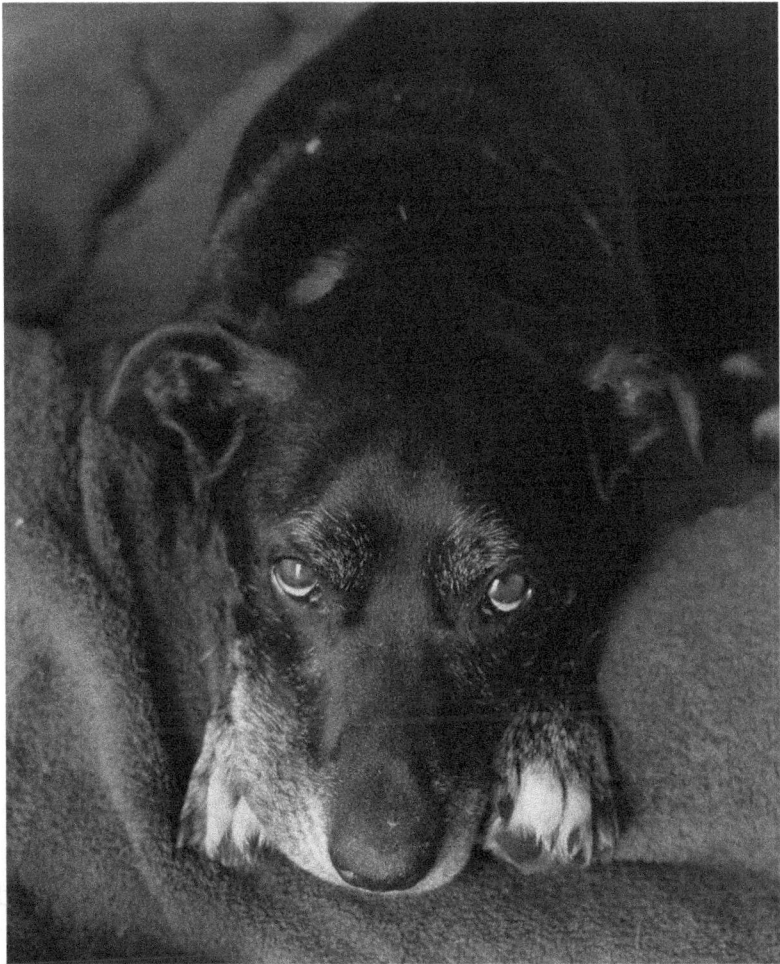

The Weight Of Loving A Dog

We didn't choose to be dog owners. Ike found us when he wandered out of the woods one day. But now that we are, I realize that it's probably a good thing that we didn't have children. I couldn't handle the stress. Our kids would have grown up coddled and fussed and protected and probably resentful towards us about it for the remainder of their lives. Or they'd still be living with us into their 40s.

Some days I feel like a confirmed bachelor might, one who has just had a tiny baby handed over to him for safekeeping for a few hours. What does a baby eat? What does he do? How do I change a diaper? *Why is he crying so much?* My family had a dog, Violet, when I was growing up, so it's not a complete mystery. We had more cats than I can count, but cats are independent. You don't need to walk a cat. But mom did all of the heavy lifting. I didn't have to worry about buying food, grooming or vet visits or caring for Violet's body when she died.

With Ike I worry that he's eating the right food, getting the proper amount of water and exercise. Not too much, not too little. Is that a slight limp or are my eyes playing tricks? He has a skin problem that we can't seem to solve despite special shampoos, ointments and now corn- and wheat-free chow. There's the heartworm pill to give him each month, the flea collar in the spring and summer and we must be ever vigilant for ticks that somehow thwart our best efforts. We've pulled burrs from out between his toes and scrubbed mud off of his nose. Once we were certain he was choking on a gopher so we pulled it out of his mouth much to his astonishment. Through our inexperience he patiently tolerates our poking, prodding, washing and hugs.

Yesterday we took Ike in to be neutered. Kel and I had agonized over the decision for weeks, even though most everything one reads and hears encourages it. He must be in pain and confused as to why and what happened. Our hearts break that we cannot make the hurt go away or even explain to him what's happening. In the long run we know it's the best thing for him. The last thing we want is for him to sire unwanted offspring throughout the neighborhood or to be lured by the siren song of the canine vixen across the road and be hit by a car.

We are not the kind of pet-owners who confuse their little furry one with a bouncing bundle of a joy called a human baby. Clearly Ike is a dog. We do not dress him in clothes nor have him wear hats or call ourselves "mommy" and "daddy," though I understand the appeal of all of those things. But we also understand that Ike depends on us just as human children depend on their parents. He will either benefit or suffer from decisions we make on his behalf. It's (with luck) a long-term commitment and that's a heavy, scary and wondrous thing.

- November 4, 2011

Ike has no shortage of nicknames, however. He's known variously as: Nutter-Butter, Pinochle, Stink Bomb, Munchkin, Pumpkin, Ikester, Ikey and The Ikeman.

The Mockingbird Returns

Long before the two humans moved into his domain he was patrolling and guarding the trees and pastures and singing his various calls and melodies from the very top of the pear tree or the utility pole near the barn. He sang to warn other male mockingbirds to stay away and he sang to attract females to the bounty and beauty of his home. Sometimes one of the humans would imitate his tune or try to suggest other sounds, but he just ignored them and continued with his clever hawk and jay and chickadee imitations.

One cold winter morning the first year of their arrival the small human came out of the house carrying a plate with shiny, jewel-bright pieces of fruit on it. From his tree top he watched as she held the plate up towards him, then placed it down on the ground, all the while singing, "maaaa-ckingbird, maaaa-ckingbird." As soon as her back was turned and the door to the house closed behind her, he flew down to the ground close to the plate and swiveled his head to assess her offering. He hopped closer and with a discerning eye, picked the juiciest pieces of cut-up grapes and blueberries. After sampling several tidbits, he flew into the holly bush to clean his bill. By the end of the day, the plate was empty.

Every morning throughout the winter and into early spring the humans came out and placed the plate on the ground. Some days the mockingbird was quite bold and let the humans come close. Some days he didn't come out until after they'd gone back inside the house. On mornings when the small human was particularly slow, he chirped impatiently and flew back and forth in front of the window to let her know he was ready to eat.

When each summer came he had other concerns and other sources of food and the plate of fruit went untouched. The humans watched year after year as he courted females and started families. Some years snakes made off with the eggs or raccoons found the nests and ate the chicks. The mockingbird would sometimes have to build two or three nests before a family could be raised. He never gave up.

On three separate occasions the humans were sure that the mockingbird had met a sad fate. Small piles of mockingbird feathers were found in the grass and they mourned the loss of their friend, but each year he reappeared. For four autumns now, including this very one, as the mornings get colder and the days shorter, the mockingbird has returned to sing from the tops of the trees and to receive his daily plate of fresh fruit, lovingly cut-up by the humans who live in his domain.

- November 5, 2011

One morning a year or so after I wrote this as I sat at my work desk that faces the large sliding glass doors overlooking the driveway and pasture, I saw a large object fly towards the glass, hit it very hard, and drop to the ground. I rushed outside to find the broken body of a mockingbird, blood pouring from its mouth. I picked up the warm body

and sat and cried, stroking its feathers. I was sure it was our friend. Kel buried the bird near the garden, one of the mockingbird's favorite haunts. We held out hope that perhaps it wasn't "our" bird that had died, but we never saw our friend again.

The Small Town Myth

I am victim to a nostalgia of my own making, fueled most likely by untrustworthy childhood memories and nurtured by stories written by people with their own untrustworthy memories. It's the town of porch swings and pies cooling on windowsills. Of twilights filled with fireflies and hearing in the distance a woman call a child into the house followed a few seconds later by the squeak and slam of a screen door. It's a town that each Fourth of July or Memorial Day adorns the street lamps with American flags, that has a Town Hall built of rough-hewn sandstone that sits solidly and silently guarding a grassy square and a white gazebo decked with giant baskets dripping with petunias. There's an ice cream shop, a diner offering real "home-cooking," a notions store and a post office that's been there as long as anyone can remember.

I've driven through and past hundreds of these towns. As a family we spent a lot of time on the road and dad preferred taking blue highways and back country roads that zigged erratically in every direction. The single main street (often called Main) appeared from between vast fields of corn and suddenly sprouted a neat row of houses and a wide sidewalk pushed tectonically here and there by the roots of the old maples and oaks. Old iron fences, painted black, decorative but unreliable guardians of neat lawns. The houses gave way to brick buildings, each with a block of sandstone at the top boasting the year they were built. In another block one is back to houses and after a half mile, deep into cornfields again.

I grew up in a small town, and although it has a town square with a gazebo, it isn't an inviting place. Two of the four corners of its main intersection have gas stations on them. Fast food restaurants line the roads. There is no sidewalk anywhere to be found. This is not to say there is nothing good about living in a small town. I prefer it to living in a large city, but does my ideal exist?

After many years living in major metropolitan areas, I again live at the outskirts of a small town. To say it lacks charm is like saying the Hunchback of Notre Dame had a minor back problem. The main street has more boarded up buildings than functioning stores. The barber at the barbershop where I used to get my hair cut (he's since gone out of business) would tell me stories of police corruption and drug trafficking. As he told it, our town is as dirty as the Chicago mayor's office. There is nothing for teenagers – or anyone else – to do. No movie theater, no video store, no bowling alley nor mall. The park is under-utilized. Work is scarce and if you're looking for amenities or good restaurants, keep heading west until you hit Oklahoma City. One or two of the town's buildings wear the charm of the distant past, but they're marred by neglect, flaking murals or fire damage. Meth is a serious problem. Recently, bottles of cold medicine were tempting enough to inspire a recent break-in at the local Walmart.

And yet my dream persists. I can't imagine I will stop seeking in one way or another the idyllic small town. In what remains of my lifetime I'll probably drive through many that offer tantalizing elements of my fantasy. But I suspect that the perfect small town is the place just out of grasp, always somewhere else, in the next state or just down the road.

- November 12, 2011

Memories Of Baked Goods Past

Just around the corner to the entrance of Roger's Grocery store, past the cashiers and the customer service desk, were the big, shining glass cases that housed tall cakes covered in thick frosting, mounds of cookies and rugulach; deep, dark brownies, pecan rolls, crumbly coffee cakes and loaves of perfectly baked bread: Hough's Bakery. It was the first place one naturally pushed their cart and the first place my mom would stop during any trip to the market. It was both heaven and hell for a child with a raging sweet tooth.

On a good day (and there were many), mom would order up two of Hough's sugar cookies and the woman behind the counter would reach into the case with a small piece of wax paper and place the cookies in the distinctive white bag printed with the blue Hough's logo. The bag was a mere formality because we tucked into the cookies immediately. They were about 5" in diameter, a half inch thick and sprinkled liberally with thick sugar crystals that fell off as we bit into the crunchy, buttery cookie. I could never make mine last long enough.

My favorite item by far, however, was the cinnamon coffee cake. I can still taste it: a dense, buttery cake generously coated with pillowy cinnamon-sugar nearly as thick as the cake itself. The corner pieces were coveted because they hosted more of the topping.

Then there was the white cake. My mom's and brother's favorite. Nothing fancy, just a beautiful snowy-white cake coated with white frosting. The flavor was subtle but it invited one to take bite after bite until the plate was, sadly and shockingly, empty.

Luckily for us kids, mom turned out top-notch chocolate chip cookies, chocolate cakes and brownies but her claim to fame (at least in the small world of our house) were her pies. I loved to watch (and "help") her mix and roll the dough. She used Fluffo, a lemon-colored shortening that, though it contained no butter, imparted a buttery flavor to the crust. Mom would cut up the scraps, top them with cinnamon and sugar and bake them up for us kids. Every time she made a crust she would declare it a disaster, but the results were always tender and flaky, the perfect complement to cinnamon-y apples, or juicy raspberries or the traditional Thanksgiving Day pumpkin.

I didn't have to be at home to partake of delicious baked goods. My best friend's mom, Mrs. P, made raspberry jam from berries picked from her own garden. The smells in the kitchen during preserving day were sweet, sticky, juicy-red summer. Mrs. P baked up something called Victorian sandwich and I asked for the recipe a few times, but never was able to get my hands on it. Between two layers of vanilla cake baked in a 9"x13" pan, Mrs. P would spread a generous slick of her raspberry jam. She served it to us along with a big frosty glass of Ovaltine.

Mrs. P passed away a couple of years ago. Mom doesn't bake much anymore and Hough's Bakery is no longer in existence (but grateful Clevelanders can still get baked goods made from Hough's old recipes at a shop on Lakeshore Boulevard). I no longer indulge in baked goods made with butter, eggs or refined flours, but my memory is good enough that I can recall the tastes and textures of those childhood treats. I wouldn't trade in those memories for anything.

- November 13, 2011

Grief Management

I'm a planner. My workout clothes are set out the night before, as are everything we will need for breakfast in the morning. I plan out the week with long to-do lists and jot down notes on calendars. I typically start packing one or two weeks before leaving for a trip. This has worked pretty well for me and for the most part, I feel in control of most aspects of my life.

With one glaring exception. How does one plan emotionally for the death of a friend or loved one? Up until recently thoughts of this kind have not intruded upon the placid rhythm of my life. I've yet to experience the death of a close family member. But, the past year has been a rocky one for both my family and myself and for several of my dear friends. Two of my friends have recently lost parents. Kin and kind have been marred by serious illness. A member of my own family came alarmingly close to losing his life and the battle is not yet over.

Yes, there are things to do: understand the wishes of those close to us, write up wills or requests, get the Power of Attorney and Advanced Care Directive in order and there is some kind of comfort in accomplishing these "administrative" tasks, if only because it takes one's mind off of the wrenching, emotional aspect of the passing of someone we hold dear.

If only there were a way to mitigate the crush of sorrow. Maybe, like taking a tiny sip of poison each day in the hopes of gaining immunity from its deadly effects, one could bear a small dose of grief everyday so that by the time the crisis comes, one isn't overwhelmed by the black and bleak weight of loss. If only that kind of planning were possible. I'm afraid even if it that small act was performed devotedly - taking that tiny, bitter dose every day - that it would never diminish the flood that comes after losing a loved one.

It is proper, I guess. The heavier the sorrow, the deeper the love. The harder the loss, the sweeter the impact that loved one had on life.

- November 18, 2011

Some Thoughts About Dirt

The other night the sky was clear and star-strewn, the moon waning but still nearly full and low and bright just above the dark line of trees. A streak of moonlight shifted and glittered along the surface of the pond and long, cool-colored shadows lay down past tree and fence and barn.

A strong breeze blew from the south, balmy as a late spring day and with the same sense of expectancy and possibility. With it came the moist and cool smells of earth. The odor of the earth respiring. The same dirt furrowed by gophers, churned by cows' hooves and dug and turned with shovels by us humans to house and nourish our kale and turnips, tomatoes and sunflowers and bee balm.

We filled our lungs with the rich smell, displacing, we imagined, whatever bad and sour and unhealthy may formerly have been residing there. The incongruous smell of spring on the cusp of winter.

- November 19, 2011

Movies with Mom

Though sometimes I didn't think so, I was lucky to be the youngest of four. I did suffer the "slings and arrows" of teasing and having food filched off of my plate by older siblings because I was "little," but I also benefited from the experiences of my siblings and from having built-in playmates and companions. Sharing a small bathroom was tough, but it taught me something about compromise and cleanliness. At least I think it did.

But being the youngest meant that eventually, as my siblings grew up and spent more time with friends or doing other activities, they needed my parents' attention less and less. I was there to soak it all up. One way that manifested itself was in movies.

Usually it was me and both parents who headed out after dinner to see the latest films, but on nights that my dad was away traveling, mom and I would often plan something special. After a quick dinner out, we'd drive to one of the revival movie houses in Cleveland, the Cedar-Lee or perhaps the cinema at Case Western Reserve University. Mom picked the classics, movies that she had loved as a younger person and remembered fondly.

Close on the heels of having finished the epic book, *Gone With the Wind*, we drove down to Cleveland, fortified ourselves with popcorn and candy and tucked into the worn magenta-colored velvet seats at the Mayfield Theater in Little Italy to watch the four-hour film on the big screen. What a beautiful sight! The costumes and characters, the plantation houses, the raging fire in Atlanta - and gorgeous Vivien Leigh. She embodied Scarlett and I thought she was the most beautiful woman in the world.

I can still smell the buttery-popcorn aroma as mom and I

147

walked around the lobby working the kinks out of our legs during the intermission.

Then there was *The Red Shoes*. Another tortured romantic drama that didn't end so well. This was during the height of my Mikhail Baryshnikov obsession so a ballet-themed movie was perfectly suited to a moody, besotted teenager. I remember the vivid, garish colors of the film and wondering why the doomed heroine didn't ditch her wafty, whining boyfriend and just happily dance herself to death with those magical red shoes!

One of mom's more interesting choices was *La Strada*, a Fellini film. I struggled a bit at first with the subtitles, but found myself completely drawn into the bizarre and tragic flavor of the film. It haunted me for days afterwards.

How would these films hold up today? *GWTW* remains one of the few movies that has aged well and also lives up to the complexity and spirit of the book. *The Red Shoes* and *La Strada* would probably not stand up to second viewings, but it doesn't matter. I don't need to see them again. What was and what remains priceless was having that one-on-one time with my mom, finding out a little something about her and imagining what she might have been like as a girl my age. Chances are good that she had been just like me, besotted and moody.

- November 26, 2011

DECEMBER

The Dream

In his dream he sees his father riding on horseback across the fields that have taken on the bright, glowing green associated only with dreams and with afternoons that carry thick, gray storm clouds across the sky without letting them release their rain. The beautiful green fields are smooth and flow without blemish to the horizon. Even through the unbreakable drift of the dream, he - as the dreamer - feels the desire to roll down the slopes, to feel the cool grasses along his bare arms, against his face, and the hard earth beneath, gently prodding him along spine and shoulder blades with its moist clumps.

In the dreamworld, his father rides across the fields, returning home from a journey that has taken him away for many months. His jaw is covered by a thick beard and about him seems a haze, the hesitant indefinite color of dust kicked up by a slight breeze. Soft brown dirt that has traveled the miles with him covers the horse, coats his leather chaps, his unruly hair and makes the green of the landscape seem even stronger and cleaner. His father and the horse never waver from the invisible line that brings them closer to home, but he looks off in the direction of far off trees and at the ripples, one after the other, of small hills.

His father rides across the land. It is *his* land and trees and grass are allowed to grow without limit or constraint. Wild and free. It is this way because the boy's mother would have it so and his father loves his mother above anything else. The boy's dream progresses and the man and horse have now reached a thin dirt road that trickles into the distance. Before it disappears it passes by a large bed of flowers. Against the glowing green, below the dark gray sky, the flowers' colors explode among the plain grasses. Yellow seeming to be the brightest and the most burning, until the eye catches the flame-lick of red, then vibrating plumes of purple.

His father does not pause at the flowerbed, even though it is his wife who has loved the flowers into existence, but turns his horse onto the thin road. On his left side the tamed arms of dozens of apple trees reach up and into thick leaves and the tiny pale buds of infant fruit grow bigger in the still of the day without the notice of the man on the horse.

The road dwindles to nothing and he is again riding on smooth grass and a gentle slope that pulls him towards his house. A breeze - nothing more than a whiff if wind - causes the boy's father to twitch his head to rid his eyes of the strands of hair that have fallen across his forehead and as he does, he sees the color gray, as brooding as the clouds, floating among the green leaves. He recognizes the color instantly, the diaphanous quality of the plain fabric. It is his wife. His wife has hanged herself, dressed in a sheer sheath, from the branches of one of her apple trees.

For a second his father's pale, pinched face is visible and then the face disappears as he turns his body and reaches for - pulls out and swings towards the body of his wife - a large, shimmering blade. The blade slices through the rope that supports the body of his wife and she falls across the brown back of the horse. The knife disappears and the boy's father holds the body as he continues riding across the green field towards home.

- December 1, 2011

This story came to me in the form of one of the most vivid dreams I've ever had in imagery, color and subject. I feel as if it wrote itself. This was one of those dreams that haunts for days afterwards.

151

The Name Begins with the Letter W

Oklahoma seems to have an inordinate number of towns beginning with the letter W: Wetumka, Weleetka, Wichita, Watonga - for a start. If they sound as if their origin is Native American, your ears haven't deceived you. Before Oklahoma became a state in 1907, it was known as the Indian Territory and then the Oklahoma Territory and was where numerous tribes found themselves after being co-erced, marched, treatied, tricked and pushed out of their an-cestral lands courtesy of the Indian Intercourse Act of 1834. Drive along I-40 or almost any other major road in Oklaho-ma and the tribe names tick off one after the other on green road signs, one reservation ceding to the next: Chickasaw, Sac-Fox, Seminole, Muscogee (Creek), Shawnee, Choctaw, Cherokee and on and on.

Not far down the road from us is another town beginning with the letter W. It's the county seat of Seminole County, but if you didn't know better, you'd expect that someday soon it would dry up and blow away, like a brittle Black Jack oak leaf in late autumn. Down Route 56 as you come into town from the north a proud stone house sits high above the road, a large estate with tall pecan trees and manicured, rolling hills that ease you towards muddy pastures where a small herd of buffalo graze alongside a couple of llamas and a few head of cattle. A half mile further and just past the bridge is a bright lime green building slowly sinking and decaying into a parking lot. It was once a Chinese restau-rant. A mortuary sits across the road and then a gas station and a liquor store. A large cinder block building looks im-penetrable until you see the huge gaping hole where the roof collapsed. At the stoplight, if you look to your right out your car window you'll see the remnants of an old motel, the open windows and doors black and empty.

On the left, an enterprising couple has renovated a 1940s

era gas station and now they sell plants, fruits and vegetables. Piles of bright orange pumpkins are stacked on bales of hay. Across the way a new restaurant has opened, offering home cooked meals. There's the gun and pawn shop, another closed gas station, Moore's IGA with a nearly full parking lot and the Sonic Drive-In which is the most successful business in town. A half block further the Black Sheep Drive-In - Sonic's competition - sits abandoned, *Sorry We're Closed* and *For Sale* signs sharing space in the same window.

There's a Daylight Donuts just past the next stoplight, then a tiny liquor store with mesh screening covering the door and windows. A neat and clean orange-painted Mexican restaurant with a sign that blinks with hope: Open. Then the retail gives way to the residential - tiny homes, some immaculate, some threadbare - stone, clapboard and several signature Oklahoma-style houses constructed of honey-colored brick with steep-pitched roofs, gables and curved doorways that look designed by and for elves. There are rusting cars, heaps of garbage, dogs on chains, abandoned toys and neat gardens filled with the brown remnants of the summer garden.

This W-named town could be a stand in for dozens of Oklahoma towns that cling to existence. It eerily resembles the town I currently call home, also a county seat. But there is enough life yet to keep it going. The old generations linger here, unwilling or unable to relocate and the younger generations - white and Native American - stay on. Family ties, the comfort of what is known and the pull of their homeland keeps them rooted here.

- December 2, 2011

Before It Snows

I love an unsettled fall day, when the wind blows hard from the northeast - cold, but not yet cold. The leaves that scuttle and scratch behind me as I walk. As clattering and nearly as unnerving as a poltergeist. When you look back, you see nothing.

Sunlight is yesterday's yellow memory. Bloated, low-hanging clouds labor slowly across the sky while a plume of fast-moving and pure white clouds, like puffs from a steam engine, speed along the horizon line. Icy drops of rain tap on shoulders, the patter increasing for a brief deluge, then stopping again in an instant. Following the dog's lead I lift up my head to sniff the air. Even my ill-equipped human's nose scents intrigue on the wind.

The earth feels spongy and soft. Among the brown and dead tufts, tender and bright green blades of cold-weather grass flicker in the wind. Pairs of ducks flush from the pond, rising with squeaky protest, pulling, pulling against gravity. They circle, hoping I'll leave so they can return to the dark gray water and the reedy shelter of the rushes along the bank.

- December 4, 2011

The Point of Rocks

In the early spring of our first year in Oklahoma, when the trees were still bare but the air had the sweet smell of impending new life, the previous owner of our ranch came over for a visit and took us to a spot near a small spring where there was a flat rock once used by Native Americans as a grinding stone. Sure enough, the otherwise inauspicious-looking rock had the unmistakable marks of man's hand. There were two shallow, smooth indentations worked into the rock, one slightly deeper than the other. How many years had it taken to engrave those marks? It felt slightly surreal to run my hands into the hollows, picturing others sitting where I was, imagining dry kernels of corn slowly pulverized into meal. I've tried many times to find the grinding rock again, but have failed. The old man had taken us right to it without a second of hesitation. Now it seems to have vanished into the woods, hidden under the deepening pile of fallen leaves and the thick, tenacious vines with wicked thorns. History slipping away.

The ranch is full of rocks and stones, of course. Mostly crumbly sandstone covered in carpets of moss in an array of complex, luxuriant greens. There is a long outcropping of rocks, a thick, broken seam that runs across our property. We learned that long ago, maybe 50 or 60 years back, rock was quarried from the ranch and used to build the local high school stadium. Looking at the size of the structure it's surprising that any rocks remain here on the land. It is an impressive if inelegant stadium, rough and sturdy, with colors ranging from deep brown to rust to burnished gold. The raw rocks hewn and hauled and fitted into place for a particular need. The hand of man touching stone.

- December 11, 2011

Getting Lost: A Christmas Story

It was Christmas Break during my freshman year in college and after a mere 3 months on my own, I was feeling quite confident and independent and adult, so when my mom suggested that my older brother and I drive out to the tree farm in northeastern Ohio to cut down an evergreen for the holiday - the farm where we had for years been harvesting our family tree - I assured everyone (*no problem!*) that I knew exactly where the farm was located. There was no need for written directions or anything so superfluous as a map. It was, I told them, *impossible* for us to get lost.

My brother was entrusted with a saw and the keys to the big gray van that had been emptied of its maroon-colored pleather passenger seats in anticipation for the fat evergreen that would soon be loaded into it. Our journey began on the back roads of rural Ohio, thin dirt roads crusted with ice and snow that refused to melt and lined on either side by tall, bare hardwoods. We cruised through Amish country and rolling brown hills dotted with big barns and clean white houses with the curtains hung diagonally across the windows. It was a frigid, gray, dull day and despite the cranking heater in the van, we were chilled. The cavernous van swallowed all of the warmth and left none for us.

At last we came to the divided highway that would take us past the tree farm. I knew that it would be on our left, but beyond that I suddenly wasn't so sure. I expected that a big sign would point us in the right direction, but as the time and miles slipped away and the sky turned a deeper gray tinged with silver, I realized that I had no idea where the tree farm was. When we drove past the *Welcome to Pennsylvania* sign, my heart sank and I turned to my brother with shame and embarrassment and admitted that I had no idea where the farm was.

Instead of being upset or teasing me, he simply turned the van around and headed back in the other direction. Evening was almost upon us and we knew our parents would wonder what had taken us so long. We couldn't possibly return empty-handed. As we drove, we kept our eyes open for another place to stop and get a tree but suddenly the road seemed depressingly empty. Dark purple and gray appeared along the edges of the sky and just as we were about to give up hope, we spotted a small sign for "you cut" live Christmas trees. My brother turned onto the gravel road and then onto a narrow driveway that took us to the front of an old farm house. A teenager came out, pulling on his coat. He led us out into the snow past rows of fledgling pine trees and farther into a field where the older trees grew tall and sturdy in neat rows.

We selected a tree and my brother got to work, lying down in the snow to get at the tree's trunk. The teenager stood with his hands deep in his pockets and watched. The wooshing sound of the saw was the only thing to be heard on that frigid early evening and after several minutes, the tree was free and we began to drag it back towards the van. My brother's coat was covered in snow on one side. We paid the young man and started back for home. I dreaded getting back and having to admit to my parents that I hadn't known where the original tree farm had been, despite my boasts.

But when we got home, my parents had not yet returned from work. My secret was safe for the time being. My brother turned to me and said, *"We don't need to tell mom and dad."* Relief and gratitude washed over me. I have no idea whether or not my brother eventually told my parents, but neither said anything to me about. As far as I knew, it remained our little Christmas secret.

- December 16, 2011

Lost...And Found

We took a walk into the woods to enjoy the beautiful late afternoon sunlight and warmth, crunched through the fallen leaves and ducked under branches with Ike and Winston running erratically ahead, exploring. We climbed up a small, rocky ridge and started to come back down when I said, *"Look for that rock with the grinding holes in them - -"* and no sooner had I said it then Kel was bending down and wiping wet leaves off of the surface of a large, flat boulder.

Sure enough, he'd found the grinding rock. One of the holes is about 5 inches in diameter and 4 inches or so deep. Moss has crept to the edge of it as if peering in. The other hole was filled to the top with years of leaves blackened and turning soupy at the bottom. It is probably 6 inches in diameter and maybe 10 inches deep. A well-used spot. I'm so glad that the grinding rock hadn't vanished after all.

When we'd cleared away the debris, Winston climbed onto the rock and dipped his head down into the large hole and drank up the water that had collected at the bottom.

- December 19, 2011

A Flea in Winter

Marke but this flea, and marke in this,
How little that which thou deny'st me is;
Me it suck'd first, and now sucks thee,
And in this flea our two bloods mingled bee;

- From *The Flea*, by John Donne

I awoke the other morning to discover a bright red con-
stellation of bumps all over my back and a sprinkling of
the same on my legs. *Uh oh.* The moment I saw them, they
immediately commenced to a terrible itching. *It's bloody cold
outside*, I thought, *what on earth could be biting me?* By rights,
all biting critters should have been wiped out by the killing
frosts that have swept through the state. They tortured me
all summer, the wretches, couldn't they leave me in peace
for a few months?

As I pondered the origin of the bumps, a dreadful image
invaded my thoughts. A specter so awful as to make me
want to run and hide from the mere idea. Once thought, it
could not be un-thought and it suddenly seemed so obvious.
I remembered that a few weeks back I had stayed at a hotel...and some hotels are apparently the safe haven of those
most heinous and skulking and cowardly of creatures. The
blood-sucking succubi, the disturber of peaceful slumber:
the lowly bed bug. Could I have unwittingly freighted the
fiends back in my suitcase to Oklahoma?? *No!*

Just a few days prior to acquiring my scarlet road map of
bites, a friend had told me that she was reeling from an in-
festation of the parasites and was in the midst of banishing
them from house and home. The coincidence of the thing!
Could it be that I too had fallen prey?!

In between scratching, I researched my enemy. Bed bug sites
abound on the internet. First I did a quick check on BedB-

159

ugRegistry.com. The hotel had not been cited for bed bugs. Phew. I learned about the hallmark sign of the bedbug, the tell-tale "breakfast, lunch & dinner" bites: three bumps in a neat row. I found out that 60% of people bitten have no reaction at all but for those that do, well, let's just say that the photos were not pretty. I learned that bed bugs can go long periods between feasts and that they scuttle off to dark corners come morning or the beam of a bright flashlight as if ashamed of their own handiwork.

I peered into the deep pile of the carpet. I lifted pillows and checked our bedding. All looked innocent. And then I checked the sheets again. I was just about to holler 'nuff when something told me to take a closer look. And that's when I saw it. Something small and brown and moving and dare I say, hungry-looking. I called for the magnifying glass. I called for back-up. I leaned in and peered into the thick glass. The hideous creature loomed large and distorted and then, sensing the game was over, it leapt with all of its might to escape my gaze and my grasp. And that's when it revealed to me its true nature. Not a bed bug at all, but its wretched and more easily exterminatable cousin, the flea.

Do not ask me how a flea came to reside alongside us in bed. No doubt he hitched a ride on Ike's toasty body and finding the temperature in the house quite to his liking, decided to set up shop and get to work. It was his undoing. With a movement as swift as a sword raking through the air, I snatched the interloper and sent him swirling down the sink drain. Take that you robber, you thief! Be gone from here and trouble us humans no more! I hope you remembered your life jacket!

- December 20, 2011

Part of the Pack

Just up the hill from my small Georgetown apartment was a large park with several grassy areas, tennis courts and woods with a stream running through it where one could take a break from the concrete. No surprise that it was a popular place for the local residents to bring their dogs. In the early mornings and in the early evenings, the park was filled with running, catching, barking and fetching dogs and their obedient humans.

Unaccompanied by a canine companion, I could walk through the park as if invisible. On the few occasions when I had custody of a friend's dogs, however, suddenly I became quite noticeable. The leash, the collar, the wagging tails were my passport, the secret handshake that grants entrance into the private club. Fellow dog walkers and owners came over to say hello and chat. With two dogs trotting close to my heels, I was immediately embraced within the doggy community.

Something similar and equally interesting has happened now that Kel and I are dog owners. We do not have a public park nearby, but when we bring Ike with us on errands, people want to come over and meet him (it doesn't seem to matter that Ike really isn't interested in meeting them). Saying hello to Ike is an introduction to us and usually a segue into a long conversation.

Doggy aunts and uncles have appeared out of the woodwork. Friends and family members keep telling us how happy they are that we finally have a dog. They sound almost relieved. Most can't believe it took us so long. How could we live on a big ranch and not have a dog and if not a dog, at least a pet of some kind? What, exactly, had been wrong with us? Unbeknownst to us (but common knowledge to everyone else, apparently) something big had been missing

161

from our lives. Suddenly, Kel and I, by the simple virtue of having Ike, became more human.

- December 27, 2011

JANUARY

Christmas In the Back Country

This was quite different. An enormous gulf was between me and the world. This was a different universe – withered, desert, lifeless; a fantastic universe where the presence of man was not foreseen, perhaps not desired.

– Maurice Herzog, *Annapurna*

Fifty-eight years before Christopher McCandless hiked into Alaska to find himself (but died before completing the process), 20-year old Everett Ruess wandered through the forbidding and desolate south central and southern Utah backcountry and disappeared. A hunter found Christopher's body, but Everett was never found, though people have been searching for him ever since he vanished. There were a few tantalizing clues: Everett's two mules were found tied up at a site where he'd camped and in a letter to his parents he wrote: *As to when I shall visit civilization, it will not be soon, I think* – and the name Nemo was discovered scratched into rock in several places. Nemo ("no man" in Latin) was the name Everett took to calling himself. Ugly rumors circulated through the town in which he was last seen. Some thought that Everett was murdered by cattle rustlers. He might have fallen from a cliff or gotten trapped in a slot canyon. Or maybe he just wanted to disappear.

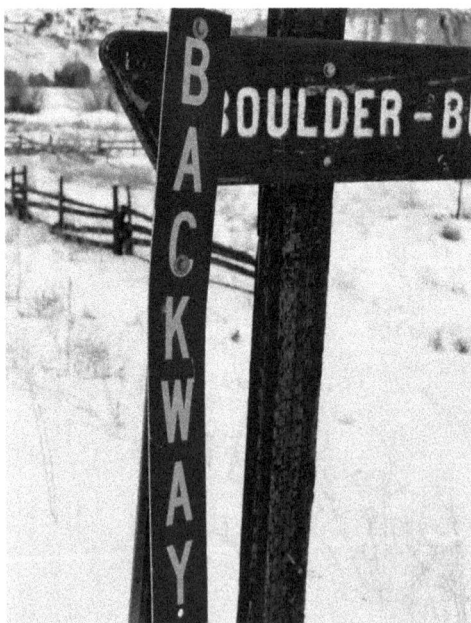

I read about Everett a while back. It's just the kind of story that fascinates me. I don't have a risk-taker bone in my body, but I'm drawn to the lonely canyons, the red rock and slick rock, the twisted junipers, the colorful arches, fins, hoodoos and searing blue skies of southern Utah. Combine that with a real life mystery and I'm hooked like a Lake Erie Walleye. Kel and I spent Christmas in the thin air of Boulder (Utah) without realizing until later that we were in Everett country. Boulder and nearby Escalante were Everett's last known stomping grounds. He disappeared into the massive Grand Staircase-Escalante National Monument that encompasses a mere 1,880,461 acres of pitiless landscape. It's no wonder his remains were never found.

In addition to hiking in the Boulder area, Kel and Ike and I made our slow way home via Kodachrome Basin and Bryce Canyon. One huge advantage Kel and I have discovered about traveling here in the winter is that there are few other fools willing to do so. It's possible to have stunning trails and sprawling National Parks all to one's self.*

- January 2, 2013

*With the exception of Bryce Canyon which was teeming with visitors. At 7 degrees Fahrenheit accompanied by a bone-chilling wind, it was an astounding sight to see cars lined up at the entrance point.

A Trip to the DMV

I happened to take a close look at my driver's license the other day and noticed that four years had passed since I'd first gotten it and it was due to expire in a month. That meant a trip to the local DMV.

A few years ago that thought would've plunged me into curl-into-the-fetal-position despair. If you have not had the opportunity to spend time at the DMV in our nation's capital you have missed out on one of life's more, um, interesting experiences. It is a circle of hell. Remember the "waiting room" scene from the movie Beetlejuice?

It is a fact that you will never, ever bring the correct combination of documents with you the first time you go. After eons spent in a long, twisting line filled with grumbling citizens, the sentry at the gate will turn you back, guaranteed. Cajoling and flattery will do nothing to break the impasse. She has a heart of stone and eyes of ice. You could have studied up on the accepted list of documents listed on the DMV website, but alas, that will have done you no good. It's nothing less than a shell game. Best to bring along a passport or two, letters of recommendation from friends in high places, various unopened bills, elementary school report cards, a certified birth certificate (don't even think about bringing a copy), a note from your mother, your Sam's Club membership card and a bouquet of flowers (better hope you bring her favorites) for the sentry. She'll fix you and your pathetic pile of paper with a hard, beady stare and if you're lucky, motion you on. Do not hesitate. Grab the pitiful detritus of your life and go.

Once past this first line of defense be prepared to wait. Your tender buttocks will be resting in chairs the hardness of which would challenge the Buddha's peace of mind. You will be waiting with the masses: the tired, the unwashed, the re-

166

signed and a few close to blowing a mental gasket. Numbers and letters, the meaning of which will forever be obscured to you, will flash from time to time from various screens around the waiting area. Although there are plenty of "service" windows, most of them are black holes, devoid of anyone looking remotely work-oriented behind them. They are Potemkin windows that have never nor will ever function. Instead you will witness much scurrying just beyond the glass and a determined avoidance of eye contact.

When you finally reach one of the functioning windows your waiting is not over. Your papers will be scrutinized with a dedication last seen by a forensic scientist comparing fingerprints lifted from a crime scene. There will be shuffling of papers and feet and deep sighs. Undoubtedly your attendee will come across something for which he or she has never encountered in their 25 years of service at the DMV, and so managers, supervisors and co-workers must be summoned for whispered consultation. There will be furtive glances in your direction. For a while, it looks as if you will be turned away yet again. Finally, however, papers are stamped, information has been verified, fingerprints scanned and eye tests given. It remains only to exchange legal tender for the small, flimsy rectangle of plastic.

Thankfully those days are behind me. The DMV in town is located in a cozy white building with blue shutters. A kindly older woman with laugh crinkles around her eyes stands behind the counter. She actually smiles when you come through the door and makes small talk. Around the holidays she wears those splashy sweaters sewn with sparkly thread and sequins. Photocopies of photographs of her children and grandchildren are taped to the wall behind the tall counter. There is a lighted potpourri candle and jars of locally-gathered honey for sale. When she has an errand that calls her away from behind the counter, a handwritten sign is posted on the door, such as: *"went to OKC to get stitches out. be back tomorrow.*" She works with a calm efficiency reminiscent of a mime effortlessly juggling imaginary plates and balls.

No stone-faced sentry. No mysterious signs flashing numbers and letters. Just friendly service. Washington, D.C. could learn a thing or two.

- January 2, 2012

Handwork

Let's do some math. For the sake of my numbers-challenged brain, I'll keep it simple. We live on a 160-acre ranch. There are 6,969,600 square feet in 160 acres. There are just two of us living on this chunk of earth, yet Kel and I persist in what one local calls "handwork." That is, relying on our own arms, hands, legs and energy to do both light and heavy lifting around those 160 acres. We do not own an ATV or a bulldozer or a back hoe. We have shovels, rakes and various kinds of clippers and saws, though. There is a big John Deere tractor in the barn and a couple of lawnmowers, but they are employed only occasionally. Kel and I really prefer to walk the ranch and get after some kinds of work without benefit of machine.

One of the things we do by hand is cut down cedar trees. I know it sounds sacrilegious to hack down trees and in many instances, that is the correct assumption. Here, however, cedars are considered an invasive species. They pop up like, well, weeds, aided by birds snacking on the blue berries that appear in abundance in the fall. There are clusters of cedar trees in various stages of growth around older trees. Birds sit in the branches and the seeds drop and the seeds germinate. Cedars are also water gluttons. In a parched land, the water needs to go to the species that really need it like the grass in the pasture, the stately oaks and the elegant pecans. And finally, cedar trees harbor ticks. There shall be no safe harbor for ticks while we have something to say about it.

So we are making our way around our 160 acres, on foot, with clippers in hand. Kel and I go around snipping little cedar tree babies and sawing down the older ones. Conveniently, once snipped a cedar does not grow back.

We've made noticeable progress, but the work is never-ending. I find it strangely satisfying. Not only the cutting of the trees, but seeing the piles of dead cedars become well-insulated dens for rabbits and opossums and armadillos and who knows what other creatures. Bonus: Kel and I intimately know each and every one of our 6,969,600 feet.

- January 8, 2012

Running in Places

At some point during each run this past week, I've had to stop and pinch myself to make sure I'm really running along the Pacific Ocean, that the colorful tangle and variety of flowers are real, that those are seals and pelicans I'm seeing in and on the gray and foaming water. The only rule I have is that some portion of the morning run must be along the beach. Otherwise I take whatever turn looks interesting - skinny stairways, thin alleys, wet sea rocks.

Running is a great way to explore a new place. This is not a revelation to runners, but I'm finding this out all over again on my trip to La Jolla. Each morning I get up before the traffic on the roads and the crowds on the sidewalk and hoof it all over town. Down sand-covered stairs that lead to the water and back up through the quiet streets, admiring waves and sand, flowers and trees, homes and shops. What is drudgery at home (the daily workout) becomes something to anticipate in the mornings. The air is cool and smells of salt and seaweed and blossoms.

Running is active meditation. I think about everything and nothing at all. Problems get probed and solved. Ideas bloom or get rejected. The day gets fleshed out and breakfast becomes the most tempting and earned meal of the day.

Despite the exotic surroundings, I will be glad to get back to Oklahoma. The press of people and traffic and the constant noise of a populous place are wearing. I'm looking forward to quiet and space. But still, running here has been a joy. I've got four more days of it here in Southern California. Tomorrow I'm planning on heading in a different direction, to an area called Windansea and then maybe into the Bird Rock neighborhood. I can't wait to see what's there.

- January 17, 2012

Stone Knives & Bear Skins

"Captain, you're asking me to work with equipment which is hardly very far ahead of stone knives and bearskins."

- Spock, to Captain Kirk, from *Star Trek*, "The City on the Edge of Forever" episode

As far as treating cancer, it seems like methods haven't changed that much since my grandmother died of colon cancer some fifty years ago: heavy doses of radiation followed by debilitating chemotherapy. Sometimes it works, sometimes it doesn't. Interesting and encouraging new treatments appear on the horizon and then fade into failure and disappointment. There has been good progress in conquering some forms of cancer, but others remain tenaciously hard to beat.

My brother has been through the radiation and chemo wringer. After a year of the "gold standard" chemo, it has proved to be ineffective, so now we work our way through a list of alternatives. Meanwhile, we've kept our eyes and ears tuned to the latest research, clinical trials and FDA approvals. We have him taking a cocktail of supplements for which he needs a schedule to keep track. I encourage (unsuccessfully so far...) him to incorporate dietary changes, yoga and meditation into his treatment regimen. Any and all options are on the table.

This past week at The Santosh Kesari Laboratory at the University of California San Diego we got him started on something completely different. When my brother was diagnosed in October 2010 with glioblastoma multiforme (GBM) the family dove into the internet looking for anything we could find on treating this deadly disease. One of the things that popped up was something called the NovoTTF - described as a helmet that used electric fields to disrupt the growth of cancer cells. Real out-there stuff, but intriguing. At that time, the device was still in clinical trials, so my brother opted for the traditional treatment regimen: radiation and chemotherapy.

Sometime during his treatment the "helmet" was approved by the FDA for use in the treatment of GBM and neuro-oncologists could begin prescribing it once they were certified by the inventing company, Novocure (based in Israel). When we learned that the standard chemotherapy was not working for my brother, we immediately went back to the idea of the "helmet." Only a few clinics in the country are as yet certified to prescribe the device and San Diego was the closest one to my brother.

Long story short, my brother is now wearing the device. It is not for the faint of heart. It is cumbersome, awkward and elicits stares and sometimes polite, sometimes rude, questions. The head has to be shaved clean. The batteries are huge, heavy and last only two hours which means planning ahead even for short trips. The device beeps if it gets too hot. It beeps if the power wavers. It beeps when the battery dies. It must be worn for a minimum of 18 hours a day. It comes with a large rolling case, a large bag of redundant equipment in case something fails, and a tote for a razor, bandages, scissors, rubbing alcohol and medical tape. Long cords get in the way of putting on coats, moving quickly and getting in and out of cars. The patches that house the thermistor disks are sticky and tend to get tangled and mangled and they must be replaced every 4-7 days. No doubt this will change over the years and the device will become streamlined, but for now, it's a real pain in the ass.

There is no argument that the bigger pain in the ass is a diagnosis of GBM. So despite all of the hassles, we are grateful for this option. Despite the primitiveness of it - the "stone knives and bearskins" aspect of it we can't help but imagine what a breakthrough this device could prove to be and not just for people who suffer from GBM, but from other types of cancer (Novocure will launch a device for lung cancer next). Maybe all of this time we've been barking up the wrong tree. What if toxic chemicals and poisons aren't the answer? Imagine what a miracle it would be if cancer patients could be cured with a device that is painless and produces zero side effects.

- January 20, 2012

Who would think that a book about the history of cancer could be a page-turner? But that's exactly what *The Emperor of All Maladies: A Biography of Cancer* by Siddhartha Mukherjee manages to be. It is a surprisingly fast read, despite the subject matter. But if your prefer to "watch" your books, check out the Ken Burns documentary inspired by the book.

FEBRUARY

A Humane Society

In the fall of a year that I can no longer clearly remember, a friend and I would head out once a week in search of the best, juiciest, cheesiest hamburgers our city had to offer. We sampled sandwiches from steak houses to trendy eateries to dimly-lit holes-in-the-wall. Sometimes we'd talk about her experience volunteering at an animal shelter where most of the workers were vegan. She felt a strong judgment from them, a feeling of elitism because they didn't consume animal flesh or wear leather but she did. This feeling eventually led her to quit volunteering. As we bit into our dripping burgers, we'd puzzle and joke about their snobby behavior and ask, isn't the most important thing that she was there, helping animals?! Did her choice of food really matter?

So. Now here I am. Many years later, a plant-eater volunteering at an animal shelter. The situation is reversed. I'm the lone vegan among omnivores.

Animal shelter volunteers and employees have my respect and admiration. They work long, hard hours in an often unpleasant, noisy and odiferous environment. Much of their day involves cleaning up blood, puke, piss and feces. They remember the names of each animal that has passed through their door and they hide tears of both joy and sadness when an especially beloved furry friend has been adopted and leaves for their (hopefully) forever home. They interface with the uncaring and the oblivious, the neglectful and the malicious. They minister to the sick and comfort the dying. They tenderly hold the cat that has been shot or the dog that has been set afire. They witness the handiwork of the ugliest and cruelest in man and they try to undo the physical and psychological damage.

And then they go home and throw a hotdog on the grill or carve into a roasted chicken.

This is the disconnect. This is where I was those many years ago when I knew that I loved animals, that I said I loved animals and yet my actions and my food choices belied that assertion. The animal shelter worker's anger is raised when the abused or neglected cat or dog or bird or horse comes under their care. How could anyone hurt or kill these gentle creatures? And yet with the items they choose to put in their shopping cart, they are causing – condoning – the pain, suffering and death of other innocent creatures.

I attempt to be mindful of not being "one of those vegans." The one who comes off as preachy, judgmental, superior – the one who seems to care for animal welfare above that of her own species. I am not that vegan. But I cannot return to the mindset of those hamburger-eating days of oblivion. If I love animals, if I respect that they have an equal place on this planet, than I cannot allow myself to knowingly cause their harm or death by consuming and using their flesh, their skin or their fur.

- February 6, 2013

The Long Shadows of Late Afternoon in Winter

"Which way should we go?"
"Let's go up."

And we do. We follow the cows' paths, smooth and slim, erratic. Some of the paths are deep gulleys with mud rivulets where rain has gushed; some are sandy and smooth. We aren't the only ones who take these byways. There are coyote prints and dog prints, opossum and raccoon, crow, turkey and large feline prints that appear secretive, slow, stealthy.

In spots the air is cooler and lighter. We squint into the setting sun that burns more fiercely as if recognizing its own sad passing below the horizon: *don't forget me*. As the hour deepens, our shadows lengthen, soon so long it is as if we are following them home.

- February 7, 2012

Winter Comes (Briefly) to Oklahoma

I bought the jacket from Eddie Bauer back in 1997 while living in Russia. Mail order is a wonderful thing. It's a man's large. Not sure what my thinking was on that. I'm 5'4" and weigh, well, not nearly a man's size large, let's put it that way. It is the warmest jacket on earth based on my vast research on cold-weather jackets employed around the globe.

The insulated overalls, which I love deeply, came from a local store called Sharpe's and are a boy's size large. Apparently women don't merit their own cozy insulated overalls. They'd probably come in pink anyway, so maybe it's for the best. Mud and cow manure don't look so good on pink. Then there's what I call a "neck gator," which can be used like a hat, scarf, or for going around incognito. Sometimes you just want to take a walk without being mobbed by crazed fans (cows). Underneath it all are long johns, sweat pants, a long-sleeved t-shirt and two fleeces. It's a wonder that I can move at all. I could be down a long time if I fell.

This is how I've met the morning for the past couple of days as a very cold system moves through the state. The forecast is for more cold and maybe our yearly ice storm late tonight and into Monday. So I'll be gearing up again at least for another day. If you don't hear from me for a while, assume the worst, and send someone over to pick me up off of the ground.

- February 12, 2012

The Body on the Road

I was the last to be dropped off that night, late. Morning, really, around 3 or 4 am. I'd been with my friends since early evening, doing nothing much. Something we did quite well. I was on the passenger side of the big, broad front seat of Gary's 50s-era car, all shiny chrome and waxy leather. He loved and babied that car so as he made the right turn off of the pavement of Wilson Mills onto the gravel road that ran past my home, he slowed down to avoid any spray of rocks pinging against the pristine paint job.

Save for the headlights there was no illumination on the road on that mild summer night. And it was quiet. Even the crickets had gone to sleep. As Gary turned the steering wheel the bright beams of the headlights swung wide and resettled onto the road and something flashed ahead of us. Gary slowed, stopped, and put the car into park. The sound of the crunch of wheels on rocks ceased. Seconds ticked by without either one of us moving as our brains struggled to make sense of the image on the other side of the windshield.

A few feet in front of the car was a limp form, human, down in the dirt, right in the center of the road. My throat constricted but my hand was reaching for the door handle. Gary was already out. We walked to the front of the car, the light flooding our faces, the body bright, alarmingly three-dimensional yet sickeningly boneless. Neither one of us wanted to reach for it.

But. A dummy. Something stuffed and dressed to look human. We looked at each other, relief mingling with the dissipating remnants of fear and dread. Thank goodness it hadn't been real. Thank goodness we hadn't run over it. Thank goodness we didn't have to help.

Gary dragged the dummy to the side of the road. My heart

180

rate slowed. We got back into the car and drove the next mile in silence, following the sturdy beam of the headlights to my house, dark and comforting in the early morning.

- February 17, 2012

He Looked Like Jesus

Wendover, Nevada. Dry and brown and sparsely populated. At least back in the 1980s. Hardly a destination town unless you were from Utah and you were looking to get a beer stronger than 3.2. Or you wanted to lose some money.

The four of us sat in the sky-blue Pontiac Bonneville in the parking lot of the casino in Wendover. The engine refusing to turn over. Refusing even to make that sad *click* when the battery is nearly dead. It was very late. The plan had been to spend a few hours in the casino and then head back across the Bonneville Salt Flats, back to Salt Lake and to sleep. It didn't look like that was going to happen.

My brothers had poked around under the hood and determined that the alternator was shot. There had been no hint of trouble when we'd left Salt Lake late on a bright, sunny afternoon. Where were we going to get an alternator at two in the morning in a deserted border town?

It didn't occur to any of us to pool together our meager funds (credit cards? we didn't have those), get a couple of hotel rooms and leave the problem-solving for the sunlit hours. So we sat, thinking of what to do next. We didn't see the man come up to the car. All of a sudden there he was, peering into the driver's side window, tapping his finger on the glass. Startled, my brother's head reared back. The lights in the parking lot had turned the stranger's face yellow, his hair into a bright halo. The man spoke through the glass, *"Do you need some help?"*

The man looked like Jesus. Or, rather he like the classic depictions of Jesus: tall and thin with long brown hair, a long beard. My brother replied and the man said, again through the glass, *"I know where you can get one."* It seemed utterly preposterous, but they were the words my brother needed to hear, and so he opened the door of the car. The man's voice was clear now, loud, since glass was no longer separating us. *"I can take you there right now."* Without so much as a glance into the back seat where my other brother and I were sitting, Jesus and my brother walked away and disappeared into the dark.

I was certain that I had just seen the last of my brother. No good could come of a stranger tapping on a car window during the darkest, the most unsettled hours of the night. Yet we all sat completely immobile. It seemed to me we could have sat there, unmoving, throughout the night, into the next morning and deep into the next day. I'm sure the three of us remaining in the car spoke, but I can't remember what was said.

It seemed as if hours had gone by, yet the sky was still black when again, out of nowhere, a person walked up to the car. My brother. Alone. He opened the driver's side door. Cradled in his hand like a surgeon gingerly carrying an organ meant for transplant, he held an alternator. The boys got out of the car and went to work under the hood. Then they were finished and my brother turned the key. The engine sounded weak, the patient slowly coming to after surgery. The dash lights flickered and died. But the engine eventually turned over and we rolled cautiously out of the parking lot and headed east, back into Utah. We discovered that to keep the car running there could be no dash lights, no radio, no rolling the windows up and down. The Salt Flats stretched out on either side of the road, eerily bone white even in the dark.

As we drove, my brother told us what had happened. I will leave the details for those of us in the car that night. And to Jesus, of course. Suffice to say that after they found the part that was needed, my brother gave him a few bucks and Jesus

183

walked back into the night and disappeared.

- February 24, 2012

MARCH

Back to My Plow

Every once in a while I get the itch to be in a city. When I get tired of wearing work boots, dog-hair-covered shirts and dirty jeans. When I just need some time in a store that isn't Walmart. One that's stocked with extravagances like tempeh, miso and fresh fennel. When a thin layer of lipstick makes me feel made up like a beauty pageant contestant.

I got my big city fix last week in one of the country's most beautiful cities, San Francisco. There is no doubt there is something exhilarating about being in a large metropolitan area, the streets and highways like pumping arteries, the overwhelming amount of goods and services - anything that one's heart desires. The flow of people from every walk of life and culture making their way along sidewalks and through city parks. New vistas, unfamiliar sounds. I enjoy it all and sometimes feel like a country bumpkin fresh off of the turnip truck, constantly swiveling my head to take in the colors and sights.

The urge to be surrounded by cement, however, and block after block of buildings and endless streams of cars passes quickly and I'm always relieved to get back to the quiet days and dark nights of the country. My mind inevitably strays, just as it did as I was crossing over the San Mateo Bridge one late afternoon, the sun sparkling on the water and the rise and fall of blue mountains far off in the distance: *This must've been really something before humans got here.* That's when I know it's time to head home and assuage my jaded eyes with the fields and trees of Oklahoma. Time to pull my crummy jeans back on and to head out with Ike into the sound of the clean wind.

- March 8, 2012

Honey Is For Bees

There is every likelihood that the honeybees swarming in and around the Bradford Pear blossoms are ours. Our Girls. Those industrious ladies who shack up in the hives Kel and I put together two years ago. I can't help but feel tugs of the maternal when I see them. There is much activity now around the entrances to the hives, guard bees on the lookout for intruders, single-minded workers arriving with pollen-laden hind legs and new bees memorizing their home with wobbly orientation flights.

There is also every likelihood that Kel and I are the worst beekeepers on the planet. In fact, I call what we do (or rather, don't do), "beehosting," rather then beekeeping. Those early hive "inspections" proved so traumatic for us and for the bees that we decided to take the less-is-more approach and allow the bees to do what they've done, unaided, for thousands of years. We no longer open the hives or blast them with smoke and we've never once harvested honey. We made that decision before we became vegans because it made sense to us that during the lean late winter months they should consume what they had so painstakingly created with all those air hours and probing of petals. Providing them with a cheap substitute - sugar syrup - didn't appeal. And we had no stomach for pulling apart their beautiful honeycomb simply because we wanted to sweeten our tea.

For the humble shelter we provide, Our Girls perform a valuable service for which we are grateful. They pollinate our fruit trees and tomato plants and zucchini. They sneak into the greenhouse and inspect the citrus plants and the basil. (They love basil.) And Kel and I enjoy watching them go about their business with absolutely no interest or concern for us. Just as it should be.

- March 11, 2012

APRIL

Mom: A Meditation on Life & Memory

Before memory there was mother. *Mom*. The one person who knew me from my minute beginnings, who nurtured me from the moment of inception, of whose existence I owe for my own.

For 50 years I have gathered experiences and they are layered one upon the other like the growth rings of a tree. Each year the trunk grows thicker with memories. Going forward those new rings will be absent of my mother. Now in the days following her passing, my head is a jumble of images. They come out of order, blurred at the edges. Like looking at stars, they are easier to discern when glancing the eye just past them. Why are our powerful brains yet so feeble in recalling the most important moments, those small, deceptively inconsequential moments that truly make up the rich, varied and flawed fabric of our lives?

I tease these fragments from the depths:
- The weak yellow glow from a nightlight in the bathroom illuminates me, an ill child, and my mother hugging me despite my sickness.

- Standing next to my mother in the kitchen as she rolls out pie dough; watching with envy at her skilled and steady fingers crimping the dough in perfect, delicate crescents.

- My mother clasping her strand of pearls around my neck on my wedding day.

- Me placing a spoon in my mother's hand – creped and wrinkled now and speckled with age spots – and gently moving that hand near a bowl of soup.

For months my mother resided in the prison of her mind and body. I don't know how much she knew of what was going on around and inside her, but I know she knew enough to want to get out. And so there is some solace in her release. The small, personal tragedy of my mother's

189

death is absorbed into the millions of small, personal trage-
dies that preceded hers over the millennia and not one of us
can avoid making our own deaths part of the manufacture of
this relentless machine. Everything that once was my mother, her memories, feelings, thoughts, ambitions, fears, and
hopes vanished in an instant. What remains now resides
under the earth in a small cemetery in northeastern Ohio.

Though I consider myself agnostic, the same sweet thought
tempts me as it did after my brother died: now my mom
knows. All the mysteries – the greatest mystery – have been
revealed to her. Does she now exist in some cool and im-
personal astral landscape or one created and tailored from
her own colorful dreams and desires? The pains and scars of
mortality are shed; lovers reunite with those dearly loved to
experience the remembered warmth of embrace, old friends
greet long gone companions to resume unfinished conversations. If this is the case then my mother is happy for she is
now with her first-born, her own parents, and friends who
left the earth before her.

Despite my age, now past the midpoint of life; despite my
unwanted status as motherless, in many ways I am still a
child. I am her child and it will always be so. Though I have
the solace of rich memories, I long for the real and living
comfort of my mother.

- April 12, 2016

Nancy Sheema Oliverio
December 28, 1933 – March 13, 2016

190

MAY

Hunting Hornworm

It's hunting season here in Oklahoma. No license needed and weaponry is just a matter of personal taste. Some of us on the ranch kill with our bare hands, but me, I don't have the stomach for the wet work. I prefer the bottom of my shoe. On The 160 we've instituted a Zero Tolerance Program (ZTP) for this particular varmint. The prey: the crafty, conniving and voracious hornworm.

Where do hornworms come from? Large (and really quite beautiful) Sphinx moths deposit eggs on the undersides of tomato leaves and the larvae eventually chew their way out of the eggs and into the green Eden of healthy, succulent tomato plants. The tiny caterpillars become fat, juicy and quite large (3"-4") as they feast on the tender leaves. They seem to love to dangle from the very tops of the plants and it takes patience to spot these critters. They are the same color as the plants on which they feed. It's the tiny spike at the ends of their bodies gives them away.

Hornworms can quickly and efficiently strip bare the branches. The caterpillars, if my shoe doesn't find them first, will molt four times before going walkabout. Then they find some nice, comfy soil, dig in, and during the final molt a green skin forms which eventually, buried, will turn hard and brown. After about three weeks, this skin splits and an adult moth emerges to begin the cycle of destruction all over again.

- May 31, 2012

DoughDirtDye@gmail.com

AnUnrefinedVegan@gmail.com

www.AnUnrefinedVegan.com

www.ingramcontent.com/pod-product-compliance
Lightning Source LLC
Chambersburg PA
CBHW050117280326
41933CB00010B/1136